HOAXERS
&
HUSTLERS

HOAXERS
&
HUSTLERS

Thomas Streissguth

The Oliver Press, Inc.
Minneapolis

The Oliver Press
Josiah King House
2709 Lyndale Avenue South
Minneapolis, MN 55408

Library of Congress Cataloging-in-Publication Data

Streissguth, Thomas, 1958-
Hoaxers and hustlers / Thomas Streissguth.
p. cm. — (Profiles)
Includes bibliographical references (p.   ) and index.
Summary: Describes the lives and schemes of noted con artists, including Lord Gordon-Gordon, Charles Ponzi, and Clifford Irving.
ISBN 1-881508-13-7 : $14.95
1. Swindlers and swindling—United States—Biography—Juvenile literature. 2. Impostors and imposture—United States—Biography—Juvenile literature.
[1. Swindlers and swindling. 2. Impostors and imposture.] I. Title. II. Series: Profiles (Minneapolis, Minn.)
HV6695.S73 1994   93-23156
364.1'63'0973—dc20   CIP
                                                            AC

ISBN: 1-881508-13-7
Profiles X
Printed in the United States of America

99 98 97 96 95 94   8 7 6 5 4 3 2 1

Contents

Introduction 7

Chapter 1   Lord Gordon-Gordon:
                The Noble Thief 11

Chapter 2   Charles Ponzi:
                The Inventive Investor 31

Chapter 3   Joseph "Yellow Kid" Weil:
                Honesty Was Beyond Him....................51

Chapter 4   Oscar Hartzell:
                The Farmer Who Milked Millions 73

Chapter 5   Orson Welles:
                The Accidental Hoax 87

Chapter 6   Clifford Irving:
                The Writer Who Faked History.........103

Chapter 7   Jim and Tammy Bakker:
                The Preachers with a Golden Touch ..123

A Chronology of Con 143
Bibliography...151
Index..153

Charles Ponzi, one of the world's most ambitious con artists, hustled everyone from Boston investors to Italian ruler Benito Mussolini.

Introduction

*G*reed is one of our strongest emotions. Human beings always want more of what they have, and most are willing to do what's necessary to get more. Some work hard; others place their trust in promises and then hope for the best. Hustlers and hoaxers can take advantage of this. Through their words, actions, and promises, they convince us of their honesty—and then take our money.

For centuries, people have been inventing confidence games. Thousands of them exist; many keep a basic idea but gradually change their form over the years to suit the times. The most common con games are the simplest, carried out by swindlers with skilled hands and sharp eyes.

In the shell game, the victim tries to find a pea under one of three shells. The hustler moves the shells quickly enough to deceive the "mark" and win the bet. In three-card monte, playing cards are arranged upside-down on a table. Two of the cards are black, and one is red. A passerby must guess which of the cards is secretly the red one. Money is gambled, and eventually lost.

Some confidence games are more elaborate and require careful preparation, good acting, and nerves of steel. They also require time, patience, and luck. But even the most complicated hustles have something in common with the shell game and three-card monte. In every known hustle, victims need to be convinced of their certain victory. All confidence games rely on a combination of persuasion and deceit.

The hustlers featured in this book were more than simple crooks or sneaky liars. They were masters of the hoax, a grand deception carefully planned down to the smallest details. Some of them planned hoaxes merely for the pleasure of carrying out a performance. One October night in 1938, for example, actor Orson Welles fooled millions of people into believing that a deadly invasion from Mars was taking place. During the 1970s, writer Clifford Irving worked hard for months to trick one of the world's biggest and richest book publishers. For Irving, the hoax was no more than a game—a game that he eventually lost.

Most hustlers have a simple goal in mind: money. Using their own self-confidence, they rely on the greed of others to carry out their plans. The biggest hustlers of all profit not from greed, but from the hopes and dreams of others. Jim and Tammy Bakker promised faithful Christians a better life, and a better afterlife, in return for generous donations—most of which they spent on themselves.

The lives of these great hustlers teach an important lesson. No matter how skilled or successful they were, and no matter how big the fortune they gained, they almost all ended up broke, in jail, or dead at an early age. Under the weight of their own greed, their games collapsed. To take their place, new hustlers are always coming around, inventing new ways to fool us. Anyone with trust and hope—as well as a little greed—can be misled by a good game of confidence.

With fancy clothes and stylish manners, Scottish swindler Lord Gordon-Gordon duped trusting people on two continents.

1

Lord Gordon-Gordon
The Noble Thief

*T*he hoax began in Edinburgh, Scotland, in the autumn of 1868. An elegant gentleman entered Marshall and Son, one of the city's finest jewelry shops. With a proud bearing and a confident voice, he introduced himself as Lord Glencairn, a member of an ancient and noble Scottish family. After examining the merchandise on display, Lord Glencairn made a large purchase, and offered a personal check in payment.

The check proved good, and the store allowed Lord Glencairn to open a credit account, which he used with great enthusiasm. Throughout the winter and spring, he bought 25,000 British pounds worth of jewelry (worth about $120,000), including several quite valuable pieces. But when he failed to appear in the shop for several weeks and failed to pay off his account, the store's owners began to worry.

Eventually, the store owners contacted the police. Lord Glencairn's account was in arrears, and the jewelers wanted the gentleman found. A search for him was soon underway. But despite the best efforts of Scotland Yard, Lord Glencairn did not reappear. In fact, he had departed for the United States with a large sum of money gained by selling the fine jewelry he had acquired at Marshall and Son.

Two years later, in 1871, Lord Glencairn—now calling himself Lord Gordon-Gordon—arrived in Minneapolis, a river port in the remote frontier state of Minnesota. Accompanied by his personal secretary and valet, Lord Gordon-Gordon took up residence at the city's best hotel and deposited $40,000 in cash in a local bank.

The arrival of a true aristocrat was a rare event in Minneapolis, a town where news and rumor spread quickly. Lord Gordon-Gordon became a familiar figure to the city's wealthy citizens, who were impressed by his fine taste and good manners. Shops were eager for his business, and hostesses vied for his company at their dinner parties.

Lord Gordon-Gordon gladly accepted invitations to mingle and dine with the rich and powerful families of Minneapolis. While making the social rounds, he met Colonel John S. Loomis, the land commissioner of the Northern Pacific Railroad. The two men soon became close friends.

Prodded by Gordon-Gordon's curiosity, Colonel Loomis explained his business to him in great detail. Railroads were making millions of dollars for their owners, but there was more to this industry than laying track and making sure the trains ran on time. The key to a profitable railroad, Gordon-Gordon learned, was the ownership and development of land along its right-of-way.

Though railroad owners could make money on land speculation, the Northern Pacific had a problem: no one was interested in buying land adjoining the railroad. The tracks ran through hundreds of miles of empty prairie in central and northern Minnesota. Towns, farms, and businesses in the region were scarce, and passenger and cargo traffic were light. So far, the Northern Pacific had returned little to its owners and investors.

Lord Gordon-Gordon offered a solution. He was an important landowner in Scotland and had hundreds of tenants who wished to emigrate to the United States. He would purchase land along the Northern Pacific line for the use of his Scottish tenants, who would build farms and settle new towns. This would lead to a busier railroad and rising land prices for Colonel Loomis and his partners. After making some calculations, Lord Gordon-Gordon declared himself ready to purchase about 500,000 acres.

Seizing his opportunity, Colonel Loomis offered his new friend and client a guided tour through the Northern Pacific right-of-way. Loomis arranged for the use of a luxurious railroad car, which would carry the two men in style. Fifteen covered wagons and 40 horses would transport the men where there was no track.

Lord Gordon-Gordon accepted this generous offer. With their aides and servants, the two men set off in the summer of 1871, leaving the city of Minneapolis behind them. The train made its way northward through plains and forests that appeared and vanished beyond the steel tracks. Lord Gordon-Gordon and his host enjoyed delicious banquets in elaborate tents furnished with oriental carpets and fine china. Whenever the opportunity arose, they set out to hunt the buffalo that roamed the open prairies. The trip was a great success and convinced Loomis that the troubles of the Northern Pacific line were over.

In the autumn of 1871, as the weather turned cold, the two men returned to Minneapolis. Lord Gordon-Gordon explained that he would travel to New York City to arrange the transfer of his money from Great Britain. The high society of Minneapolis put on a lavish party to see the gentleman off on his trip to the East.

Before Colonel Loomis bade his friend farewell, he presented Lord Gordon-Gordon with a letter of introduction to Horace Greeley, the editor of the *New York Tribune* and one of the most popular and powerful journalists on the East Coast. With Greeley's help, Loomis promised, Gordon-Gordon would easily find his way in New York City society.

But New York was not Minneapolis. America's biggest, richest, and busiest city was a tough and worldly place. Yet Lord Gordon-Gordon made an even greater impression among the New Yorkers than he had in the Midwest. He took a suite at the fancy Metropolitan Hotel and, with the help of his introduction from Loomis, quickly struck up a friendship with Horace Greeley.

Lord Gordon-Gordon's claim to own stock in the Erie Railroad, a busy northeastern line, interested the newspaper man, who often wrote about America's greedy and corrupt railroad barons. Greeley knew that Gordon-Gordon's stake in the Erie would allow the lord to easily control the upcoming election for the railroad's board of directors.

Lord Gordon-Gordon confided to Greeley that he was not happy with the rumors of fraud and mischief that were swirling around the railroad's owners, particularly a certain Jay Gould. Greeley and Gordon-Gordon agreed to join forces to save the reputation of the Erie Railroad. With Greeley's newspaper and the lord's money, they

One year after meeting Gordon-Gordon, New York Tribune *editor Horace Greeley (1811-72) ran for president. But Greeley was easily defeated by incumbent Ulysses S. Grant and died shortly after the election.*

would clean up the line and turn it into a law-abiding and profitable transportation company.

Only one man could possibly stand in their way: the rich and unscrupulous Jay Gould. Gould owned several large businesses and was not easily persuaded or fooled. With his partner, Colonel Thomas Scott, Gould owned a sizable share of stock in the Erie Railroad. His plans for the railroad were simple: earn huge profits by speculating in the company's stock and selling land adjacent to the Erie's right-of-way.

Through Horace Greeley, Lord Gordon-Gordon made a simple proposal. If Jay Gould would guarantee certain reforms in the Erie Railroad, Gordon-Gordon would throw his support to Gould and Scott at the next election.

Gould was interested, and he quickly arranged for a business meeting with Lord Gordon-Gordon at the Metropolitan Hotel. As they sat down, Gould politely asked about Lord Gordon-Gordon's background. Who was he, exactly? Why was he here?

Gordon-Gordon described his many connections to the British royal family, including Queen Victoria. In fact, said Gordon-Gordon, the queen had once sent him on a top-secret diplomatic mission to Europe. Although he had no formal position in the British government, the wealthy nobleman had conducted several delicate negotiations with European nations.

In New York City, however, Gordon-Gordon was merely a shareholder in the Erie Railroad. As a businessman, he simply wanted to make a good profit from his investment. He owned a large block of stock, and he would see to it that the railroad was better managed. To that end, he asked Gould to make certain changes in the operation of the railroad.

Gould agreed to these proposals for reform, but Gordon-Gordon insisted on having some proof of Gould's sincerity. In response, Gould offered a partnership: the two men would buy stock together and become joint owners. Gordon-Gordon politely declined the offer then made one of his own. Gould would deliver 20,000 of his own shares of Erie stock to Lord Gordon-Gordon as a good-faith deposit. In return, Gordon-Gordon would support Gould's election at the next board meeting. If Gould reformed the railroad and the company succeeded, Gordon-Gordon would return the shares. If, however, Gould failed to fulfill his promises, he would lose the stock—which was worth about $700,000.

Although the risk was entirely his, Gould accepted the offer and agreed to send for the stock certificates. During their meeting, Lord Gordon-Gordon mentioned that his efforts to save the Erie Railroad had come at great personal expense. In fact, he said, he had spent nearly $1 million since arriving in the United States, all in an attempt to improve the railroad.

Even Jay Gould (1836-92)—nationally known as a shrewd businessman—was taken in by Lord Gordon-Gordon.

It would be fair, Gordon-Gordon added, if a part of his expenses could be shared by the company. Would Mr. Gould make a deposit of $500,000 in cash and stock? Gordon-Gordon promised to keep the money and stock certificates in a safe place until Gould carried out the promised reforms.

Gould agreed and turned over to Lord Gordon-Gordon a large briefcase filled with stock certificates. As usual, Gould asked for a receipt for his property. Lord Gordon-Gordon, however, reacted badly to the request. With a calm and measured voice, he said that he would not have his integrity questioned. He pushed the briefcase back toward Gould. There would be no deal.

Surprised, Gould collected his briefcase and rose to leave. He wouldn't leave half a million dollars with a total stranger, not even with Lord Gordon-Gordon. As he walked toward the door, however, Gould began to consider the situation. Lord Gordon-Gordon was obviously a man of integrity and good breeding. Not only that, he claimed to be holding enough stock to oust Gould permanently from control of the Erie. A wave of uncertainty swept over him. Were the millions to be made from the railroad beginning to slip out of his grasp?

Gould changed his mind and agreed to accept a verbal promise. He gave the briefcase to Lord Gordon-Gordon, and they parted on friendly terms.

Gould was confident that he had struck the best possible bargain. As the days and weeks passed, however, he began to hear very disturbing rumors. Instead of hold-ing on to the stock Gould had left with him, Lord Gordon-Gordon was selling it on the public stock exchange. The shares that had been meant only for safe-keeping were fast disappearing. Not only that, the selling was driving down the price of the stock and the value of Gould's own holdings.

Gould was furious. He had been tricked! But he could do little on his own because he had no receipt for the stock and no written agreement. Gould asked Horace Greeley to call on Lord Gordon-Gordon to return the stock certificates. Gordon-Gordon agreed and sent Gould's briefcase back to him. When Gould counted the notes, he discovered only $350,000 worth of stock. The rest—worth about $150,000—was gone.

Gould swore out a warrant for the arrest of Lord Gordon-Gordon. Horace Clark, one of Gould's busi-ness rivals, put up $40,000 for bail so that Lord Gordon-Gordon could avoid jail and prepare his defense. Rather than escape to Scotland, Lord Gordon-Gordon stayed in New York to defend his reputation.

The trial began in May 1872. On the first day of the trial, David Dudley Field, Jay Gould's lawyer, wasted no time. He pressed Lord Gordon-Gordon for details of his life and his claim to nobility. At first, the lord dismissed the questions, claiming they were not relevant to the charges. But as Field continued his challenge, Gordon-Gordon realized he would have to make a convincing reply. For several hours, he entertained the jury and the court's spectators with a detailed account of his past. He offered the names of several famous people whom he claimed would be happy to vouch for him.

That night, Gould and Field sent several telegraph messages to Great Britain. The replies all told the same story: "Lord Gordon-Gordon" was a fake! Those whom he had mentioned on the witness stand had absolutely no knowledge of him. In fact, no noble Scottish family by the name of Gordon-Gordon or Glencairn even existed. The man was a complete imposter. Field prepared to have Gordon-Gordon arrested and held without bail on a charge of perjury.

Gould and Field arrived at the courtroom very early the next day. However, when the court was called to order, Lord Gordon-Gordon was absent. Knowing that Gould and his lawyer would check his claims, he had packed his bags, paid his hotel bill, and left town.

Gould immediately offered a $25,000 reward for Gordon-Gordon's capture. While New York City police searched the Metropolitan Hotel, Lord Gordon-Gordon traveled north to Canada, a British dominion that would shelter him from United States law.

Carrying part of Jay Gould's fortune with him, Lord Gordon-Gordon eventually reached Fort Garry, a remote outpost on the cold, windswept plains of western Canada. Just as he had done in Minneapolis and New York, he quickly became the talk of the town and the toast of high society—especially after hinting that he was prepared to make a sizable investment in nearby land.

For one year, Lord Gordon-Gordon lived in peace while U.S. officials carried on their search. But in the spring of 1873, news arrived in Minneapolis that a Scottish lord was spending money and living well in Fort Garry, 400 miles to the north. Minneapolis officials, who well remembered Gordon-Gordon, realized that the presence of this "Scottish lord" was no coincidence. In hopes of winning Gould's reward, Mayor George Brackett sent his police chief, Captain Mike Hoy, north to Fort Garry with a posse of sheriffs to capture the imposter and bring him back to the United States. Hoy arranged for a fast carriage and a team of horses. He arrived in Fort Garry in July and soon found Gordon-Gordon at a private home. Hoy took his man into custody and headed back toward the U.S.-Canadian border.

Brackett and Hoy, however, had failed to tell the Royal Canadian Mounted Police of their mission. Gordon-Gordon's friends in Fort Garry notified the Mounties, who stopped Hoy and his men, put them in handcuffs, and led them off to a Fort Garry jail. The Minnesotans were held without bail on the charge of kidnapping, and Lord Gordon-Gordon went free.

When Mayor Brackett heard what happened, he rode north from Minneapolis to free his police chief. But Fort Garry's officials refused all demands for the release of the prisoners and the extradition of Lord Gordon-Gordon.

Like many people, Minneapolis Mayor George Brackett (1836-1921) viewed the criminal Lord Gordon-Gordon as a national threat.

Soon newspapers in the United States were carrying stories of the torture of American prisoners by the Canadians. Mayor Brackett himself claimed that a Canadian official had demanded a bribe in return for cooperation in the matter of releasing Mike Hoy and his posse.

The U.S. public was outraged. Some people called for an outright attack on Canada. Mayor Brackett and

Loren Fletcher (1833-1919), one of the Minnesotans who helped search for Lord Gordon-Gordon, served as a U.S. congressman from 1893 to 1903.

Governor Horace Austin went to Washington to see President Grant about the matter in person. Although Grant made no promises, officials in the State Department told Brackett that there was only one solution to the problem: the Minnesotans would have to

Lord Gordon-Gordon, who had lived extravagantly in New York City, found a rustic hideout in 1873 at the Fort Garry outpost in Manitoba (now Winnipeg).

Stopping Lord Gordon-Gordon was one of the biggest challenges Horace Austin (1831-1905) faced during his four years as Minnesota's governor.

kidnap Canadian customs officials at the border and then exchange prisoners.

Soon the presses in Great Britain, Canada, and the United States were carrying the story in bold headlines on their front pages. Responding to public pressure, Governor Austin of Minnesota called on the state militia to prepare for hostilities. Thousands volunteered for duty. But before war could begin, Brackett and Austin made a last trip to see Canada's prime minister, Sir John Macdonald. After listening to Brackett and Austin's story, Macdonald agreed to grant bail to Hoy and the other Minnesota prisoners.

The case of Lord Gordon-Gordon had become an international incident. News of the scandal reached Edinburgh, where the clerks of Marshall and Son noticed a news item about a Scottish nobleman accused of fraud in New York and took a deep interest in this familiar-sounding case. The store sent Thomas Smith, one of the clerks, to Canada to investigate.

After reaching Fort Garry, Smith called on Lord Gordon-Gordon and immediately recognized his former customer. Although the attorney general of Canada refused to believe Smith, Gordon-Gordon insisted that Canada issue an arrest warrant so that the matter finally could be cleared up.

A few days later, Lord Gordon-Gordon announced to his friends in Fort Garry that he would soon be leaving. They threw him a farewell party at the house of a friend.

The party went on into the small hours of the night, and as the last guest prepared to leave, Gordon-Gordon retired to his room. Within a few minutes, a shot rang out from behind the door.

With his hoax at an end, Lord Gordon-Gordon took his own life. The money from Marshall and Son and from the private fortune of Jay Gould was never found.

When Charles Ponzi (1877-1949) realized he wouldn't strike it rich as a grocery wholesaler, he decided to hustle people out of their dough.

2

Charles Ponzi
The Inventive Investor

From across the Atlantic Ocean, North America beckoned to millions of Italians. They were unemployed and poor, but they knew they could find work, perhaps well-paying work, in the United States. They gave up everything to buy a ticket for the voyage across the Atlantic and the chance at a new life. With this chance of success, however, came the risk of loneliness and failure. Many immigrants would return to Italy as poor and as desperate as they were when they had left.

Carlo Ponzi decided to accept that challenge and arrived in the United States in November 1903. Hardworking and confident, Ponzi was sure that he would make a fortune. Soon he was working for relatives in the wholesale food business. The hours were long and the pay was low, but for the first time in his life, Ponzi was able to support himself.

Seeking every advantage in his adopted country, Ponzi quickly learned how to speak and write English. But he also learned that selling food was a tough way to make one's fortune. Within a year, the family business went bankrupt, and Ponzi was out of work.

Perhaps success didn't come so easily in the United States after all. Drifting north to Canada, Ponzi settled in Montreal, a French-speaking city in the province of Quebec. With his sharp clothes and confident manner, Ponzi soon found employment there—and the opportunity he needed.

Ponzi joined the staff of the Banco Zarossi, which held the savings of thousands of Montreal's Italian immigrants. Zarossi paid the same low rate of interest—about two percent—as the other Montreal banks. But the bank's customers trusted Louis Zarossi, the bank president, perhaps because he was Italian like them.

Ponzi became friends with Zarossi but soon discovered that his employer was in serious trouble. Zarossi had been making risky investments with the bank's money, and the cash in the vaults was quickly disappearing. To avoid a crash of the bank—and a jail sentence—Zarossi desperately needed an investor to put more cash into the bank.

After a few weeks, Ponzi joined up with Angelo Salvati, an old friend. Together, the two men hatched a complicated plan to take over the Banco Zarossi. Salvati, who was as poor as Ponzi, played the part of a wealthy investor who was ready to put $50,000 in the bank. At the same time, Ponzi and Salvati convinced Zarossi to offer *ten* percent interest, instead of two percent, to his customers. The increase would result in a rush of new deposits as the customers looked for a better return on their money.

According to the plan, before he had to pay out the interest, Zarossi would flee the city. When the depositors began demanding their interest payments, Zarossi would declare bankruptcy, and his bank's debts would be cancelled. Salvati would then make his $50,000 investment.

There was one part of the plan, however, that Zarossi didn't know about. After Zarossi safely was out of town, Ponzi and Salvati intended to take over his bank.

Expecting to return to his bank, Zarossi agreed to the plan. At first, everything went smoothly. Depositors lined up for their new accounts, Zarossi left Montreal, and the Banco Zarossi quickly closed. To complete their plan, Ponzi prepared to visit the Banco Zarossi's branch offices, where he would demand the transfer of cash to the central bank. In order to succeed, Ponzi had to look the part of a bank officer. He paid for his new clothes, his hotel rooms, and his train tickets by forging a check from one of the bank's customers.

The scheme could have worked if Ponzi had not made a crucial mistake: He had trusted Angelo Salvati. Seeking to take over the bank by himself, Salvati reported Ponzi to the police. With plenty of cash, blank checks, and other evidence scattered around his room, Ponzi didn't have a chance of defending himself. A Canadian court convicted him of forgery and sentenced him to three years of hard labor.

Ponzi's jail term gave him plenty of time to think about his future. On his release, Ponzi decided to become his own boss and drifted around the southern United States, inventing new moneymaking schemes as he went. But few of them succeeded, and none of them made much money, so Ponzi eventually went back north and settled in Boston, Massachusetts.

Boston was filled with poor, struggling Italian immigrants who were working hard to save money and build their futures. After paying their families' expenses, they would deposit their few remaining dollars into Boston's savings banks, where money earned four or five percent interest in a year. This was a slow way to earn money, and many immigrants resented the big banks and the wealthy Boston businessmen who owned them.

Ponzi felt there must be a better and faster way to make money in this land of opportunity. Otherwise, why

Canadian officials arrested Charles Ponzi—calling himself "Bianchi"—for forgery in 1908 and sentenced him to three years in prison.

not go back to Italy, where even a poor person could enjoy the warm weather and good wine? Perhaps Carlo—now known as Charles—Ponzi could show these immigrants the way.

Ponzi came up with a scheme: He would accept money from investors and double it in just three months. Instead of the low interest paid by the big, established banks, Ponzi would offer his customers 400 percent a year.

How could he possibly do this? To anyone who would listen, Ponzi explained that by luck and opportunity he had stumbled onto a simple way to make a lot of money. In fact, his plan was as easy as going to the post office to mail a letter.

Ponzi had learned that post offices around the world sold coupons that people could exchange for stamps. Thus, someone writing a letter to a foreign country could pay for the stamps needed for a reply.

Of course, Ponzi's scheme had a catch, which depended on the high inflation that was lowering the value of European currencies. Ponzi claimed he could buy reply coupons in Europe and then redeem them for a higher price back in the United States. With the extra money he received, Ponzi could buy even more coupons that could be exchanged for even more money in the United States.

The scheme was complicated, especially when Ponzi explained it in his rapid, confident, and cheerful voice. Yet he had little trouble lining up his first customers in 1919. To anyone who would listen—factory workers, ditchdiggers, office clerks, waiters, and schoolteachers—he confidently guaranteed a return of 50 percent in 45 days and 100 percent in 90 days. Within weeks, money began to arrive in the cramped, one-room office Ponzi had rented in downtown Boston.

His new business, the Securities Exchange Company (SEC), accepted any amount from $10 to $10,000. The company issued three differently colored slips of paper to investors. Green notes were for investments of $100 or less. Up to $1,000 bought an orange note, and blue notes were for those risking more than $1,000. In three months, as their notes came due, each of Ponzi's investors received an official-looking notice in the mail. The notice invited them to come to the SEC office to collect their money and, if they wished, to make a new investment.

As his company grew, Ponzi developed a network of sales agents. He offered them a ten-percent commission, meaning they could keep a dime of every dollar invested. Working in factories, shops, and restaurants, Ponzi's agents sold his colored notes to their friends, relatives, and co-workers.

By the end of February 1920, the SEC had brought in more than $5,000. New investors were signed up every day, and by March Ponzi was holding more than $30,000. Although his debts stood at $45,000, Ponzi was not worried. His investors were happy, and rather than turning in

A convincing salesman, Charles Ponzi (center, with cane) persuaded thousands of people to follow his crooked advice.

their notes for cash, nearly all of them reinvested their money in new notes. The clerks Ponzi had hired for the SEC office rarely had to pay out any money.

Believing he had finally found the road to easy riches, Ponzi began living as well as the wealthiest families in Boston. He bought fancy cars, expensive suits, and a mansion with five acres of lawn. His mother arrived from Italy to live with her famous and successful son.

The young tycoon kept busy depositing his money in two dozen banks throughout New England. Charles Ponzi knew better than to bother with postal coupons! No post office held more than a few hundred at a time, and not enough postal reply coupons existed in the entire world to finance his scheme. When an investor turned in a colored SEC note for cash, Ponzi paid off the notes with the money coming from new investors. He put the rest of the money in real estate, small companies, and banks.

Meanwhile, the debt at the SEC kept growing. Ponzi would have to pay his customers eventually—with money he didn't yet have. By the late spring of 1920, as his company's debt ran into the hundreds of thousands of dollars, Ponzi hatched an even better plan. He would close down the SEC and transfer its debts to a legitimate business. He would sell shares of stock in his new business and would balance his books with the money from the stock sale.

Ponzi had been making large deposits in the Hanover Trust Company, a prominent Boston bank. During a meeting with the bank's president, Ponzi demanded that the bank allow him to buy a large share of its stock. When the president and directors refused, Ponzi asked that they close all of his accounts and return his money to him immediately—in cash.

Ponzi knew the Hanover Trust was too small to carry that much cash in its vault. To avoid cleaning out their vaults and creating a panic among their depositors, the bank directors agreed to Ponzi's demand: They would sell him a majority of the Hanover Trust shares. The Hanover Trust Company was now under Charles Ponzi's direction.

Ponzi finally had control of a legitimate business and a chance to transfer the debts of the SEC to the Hanover Trust. Of course, he would not need to meet his debts anytime soon because money was still pouring into the offices of the SEC. A few bankers were openly doubtful of Ponzi's methods, but no one listened to them. After all, thousands of people were making money. It seemed that the entire city of Boston would soon be on Easy Street, thanks to Charles Ponzi and the SEC.

The spreading fame of Ponzi's Securities Exchange Company, however, was causing problems. Some people were forging the colored notes instead of buying them and turning them in for cash. Many investors were writing bad checks, and Ponzi's own salespeople were claiming

Because of his work at the fraudulent Securities Exchange Company, Ponzi became known as the "Boston swindler."

phony sales in order to collect higher commissions. A competitor opened up across the hall from Ponzi's downtown office and began stealing the SEC's customers with identical claims. Like Ponzi, this company promised to double anyone's money in just three months.

Yet Ponzi honored all his debts, whether they were phony or not. He knew that many people were growing skeptical of his claims and that any failure of the SEC to meet its obligations might start a panic. With his debts growing rapidly, a sudden rush by investors to redeem their coupons would ruin him.

By July 1920, the company had taken in more than $3 million in cash, but it owed more than $4 million to its investors. Ponzi was using newly invested money to pay off the notes as they came due, but how long could he keep that up? Moreover, he was having trouble transferring his obligations to the Hanover Trust or to any other legitimate business. As the summer wore on, he grew desperate to escape the growing mountain of debt.

When a furniture dealer sued Ponzi for $1 million, the SEC began to draw notice in the Boston newspapers. Now many Boston bankers and businessmen openly doubted Ponzi's claims. The bad press caused a panic at the SEC's offices. But the run on the business soon ended when Ponzi successfully met the investors' demands.

With confidence restored, a new avalanche of money descended on the SEC. In downtown Boston, a huge line of investors formed every morning in front of

Ponzi's office. The line slowly worked its way upstairs and into the main office, where thousands of investors turned over their life savings to the overworked tellers. The SEC was taking in nearly a million dollars a day.

Soon the growing size of Ponzi's operation drew the interest of the United States government. The Internal Revenue Service wanted to look at Ponzi's accounts. Troubled by rumors about the SEC, the attorney general of Massachusetts also started an investigation. Under pressure, Ponzi agreed to let the state examine his books. As a condition of the audit, the attorney general banned the SEC from accepting any more investments. Now Ponzi could take in no more money; he could only pay it out.

In the heat of the Boston summer, as the investigations and newspaper stories continued, Ponzi's financial empire began to collapse. A series of articles by Clarence Barron, a prestigious financial news editor, cast a harsh light on Ponzi's operation. Barron revealed that Ponzi was investing nearly all his cash in ordinary savings banks, which paid a mere 5 percent interest. Obviously, Ponzi could not possibly keep paying out 400 percent yearly interest when he was earning only 5 percent from the banks. The scheme was bound to fail. Barron accused Ponzi of taking advantage of local immigrants, who had little understanding of financial affairs and who distrusted banks.

Ponzi responded to Barron's newspaper stories by filing a $5 million lawsuit. But Barron and other Boston writers had already done serious damage to Ponzi's reputation. Several banks closed Ponzi's accounts, and frightened investors were redeeming their notes at the SEC. The panic grew worse after a U.S. postmaster announced that neither Ponzi nor anyone else had made large purchases of international reply coupons.

A natural optimist, Ponzi was sure that no mere investigation was going to stop him. He had enjoyed a spectacular rise, and he would stay in business. He still had control of the Hanover Trust. At this time, Ponzi came up with perhaps the most fantastic plan he had ever had. He would use the bank's assets to buy a fleet of merchant ships from the U.S. government. He would then set up his own merchant marine company and sell stock in the company to private investors. With the money paid for stock in the shipping line, he would settle the debts of the SEC, which he would quickly close down.

When they heard Ponzi's idea, the bank's directors could only look at him in disbelief. With the SEC under investigation and no new money coming into the company's accounts, Ponzi had only his name to use to raise the cash that was needed for his plan. When the directors refused to put their bank at risk, Ponzi realized his plan would never work.

Although he confidently denied Barron's newspaper articles, Ponzi was faced with angry mobs in front of

*Charles Ponzi, during one of his several encounters
with the police*

his office. Many of them had read a sensational story in the *Boston Globe* that revealed Ponzi's arrest for forgery in Montreal years ago. The story came complete with Ponzi's mug shots, taken by his Canadian jailers. Suddenly, Ponzi's investors wanted their money back— immediately.

When the attorney general completed his investigation of the SEC, he found that Ponzi owed his investors a total of $7 million. However, he had several million dollars less than that in available cash. He was bankrupt—and under arrest.

The attorney general closed down the SEC and the Hanover Trust and forced the SEC to stop making payments to the investors. The State of Massachusetts stepped in to take over the bank, but it was too late. Hanover Trust stockholders were wiped out, and the bank's depositors lost their savings. Several other New England banks holding Ponzi's accounts also failed and had to close down permanently.

Ponzi's dream of riches and a life of ease came to a swift end when the U.S. government put him on trial for fraud. Ponzi was found guilty and sentenced to five years in prison. After his release in 1924, the State of Massachusetts tried Ponzi and sentenced him to another long jail term.

Ponzi lost his house, his business, and his reputation. Despite his spectacular failure, however, he never stopped scheming. After his release in 1934, Ponzi announced

Sheriff Earl Blake (right) of Plymouth, Massachusetts, escorts Ponzi to court in 1924.

that he would soon write his autobiography. To raise money for publishing the book, he offered shares in the book to investors, whom he guaranteed a 100 percent return on their money. Few people took Ponzi up on his offer, however, and the book was never published. That year, Ponzi was deported to Italy and worked in the financial department of Italian dictator Benito Mussolini—where he secretly stole funds.

As World War II broke out, Ponzi moved to Rio de Janeiro, Brazil, where he worked as a representative for an Italian air company. But when the Brazilian police discovered that the airline was being used to smuggle goods into Italy, they closed down its Brazil office, and Ponzi lost his job. Broke and in poor health, Ponzi spent his last months in a charity ward of a Rio hospital, where he died in January 1949.

Ponzi's legacy was a new kind of financial crime: the Ponzi scheme. Through the years, hustlers have tried many variations of the Ponzi scheme—often referred to as a "pyramid game." The scams depend on an ever-larger stream of money from a growing number of trusting investors. New money is used to pay off earlier investors at high rates of interest. Eventually the money runs out, and the originator of the scheme disappears. Investors who don't collect their profits are left with only worthless promises. Although Charles Ponzi died sick and poor, his name survives whenever swindlers are making money too quickly and at the expense of their unsuspecting clients.

At age 60, Ponzi relaxes at the Copacabana Beach in Rio de Janeiro, Brazil.

Joseph Weil (1877-1976) invented a countless number of confidence games, and many of these swindles are still tried today.

3

Joseph "Yellow Kid" Weil
Honesty Was Beyond Him

*I*t was a hot and dusty summer's day. A well-dressed figure walked alone down the winding dirt lanes of the
Illinois countryside. He had a kind and trusting look,
and he was as thin and tall as the corn that grew in tidy
rows around him.

The stranger approached the porch of a square
white house. After carefully adjusting his collar and tie, he
knocked firmly on the front door. A minute passed before
the doorknob began to turn and a man dressed in overalls
opened the door.

The visitor greeted the farmer, and then he stated his business. He was representing *Hearth and Home*, a journal of rural life. Had the farmer heard of it?

The farmer was clever enough to guess immediately what the stranger wanted. So instead of making small talk, he simply asked the price.

The tall stranger was ready with his answer. "Only 25 cents a year."

The farmer's wife soon joined the two men. At first she was reluctant to buy a magazine, even one that was so inexpensive. Then the gentleman offered a set of six shining silver spoons as a bonus for buying a year's subscription.

After offering the couple a look at a sample copy of *Hearth and Home*, the gentleman made the sale. But before leaving, he drew a pair of gold-rimmed spectacles from his pocket. He had just found the glasses by the side of the road, he said.

Had anyone in the household lost this expensive pair of glasses?

No, they hadn't, the farmer replied.

"Hmmm . . . they look expensive. I imagine a reward is being offered for their return."

The gentleman then handed the glasses to the farmer, who tried them on. He glanced at the magazine, which included several pages of extremely large type. The pages looked sharp and clear. He removed the glasses and inspected them carefully. The rims shone brightly in the sunlight. The lenses were strong, without a crack or a speck of dust. The farmer considered for a moment.

"Tell you what," he said. "I'll give you three dollars and keep the glasses. I'll try to find the owner myself." The tall gentleman accepted the offer. The farmer hastily counted out his money and handed it over.

The gentleman was soon on his way. The farmer and his wife, several dollars poorer, watched him go. They held a magazine, a set of spoons, and a pair of eyeglasses. Together, their new possessions were worth about 25 cents. They didn't yet know that they had been swindled by Joseph Weil.

Weil was born in 1877 to hardworking German immigrants. He grew up in Chicago, a city growing wealthy from industry, transportation, and trade. A popular way to spend leisure time in Chicago was at the horse track. Weil was a good student who excelled at mathematics, but loved to cut his classes and sneak off to the races even though he didn't have a penny for betting.

After leaving school, Weil worked as a "collector" for Chicago's "bookies," people who took racing bets in storefronts and pool halls. The bookies, or bookmakers, would sometimes extend credit to customers they knew. If one of these customers lost a bet, Weil had to track him or her down and collect the money.

But collecting didn't pay much, and young Weil was determined to get rich, live well, and enjoy fine clothes and fine food. After meeting a salesman named Doc Meriwether in a Chicago saloon, Weil decided to quit collecting and join Meriwether's traveling medicine show.

Meriwether drove a horse and cart from one small rural town to another, offering a dark brown liquid that he called "Meriwether's Elixir." The elixir was supposed to clean out the stomach and rid the intestines of tapeworms—vile parasites. Many people believed tapeworms were responsible for their fatigue and poor digestion and were looking for a cure. Meriwether's Elixir was a strong medicine, indeed. Doc's wife made it by the gallon from rainwater, alcohol, and cascara, a laxative.

Meriwether was a showman as well as a salesman. While on the road, he hired Native Americans and dancing girls to entertain his customers. When the show was over, Meriwether would come to the front and offer his elixir to the audience. Meanwhile, his assistant Joseph Weil mingled with the people who crowded the stand.

Just as Meriwether was winding up his sales pitch, Weil would step forward. In an emotional voice, he would tell the sad story of his own struggle with the dreaded tapeworm: He had become tired and lazy, and unable to work, eat or enjoy life. His crops had been failing and his bank account had slowly sunk to zero. His family was suffering from constant hunger and was in danger of losing everything.

Then, he explained, he had tried a bottle of Meriwether's Elixir. The medicine cured him of the tapeworm, brought him back to good health, and saved his family.

In gratitude for the young man's fervent testimony, Meriwether would offer Weil two bottles on the spot, absolutely free. Immediately, the crowd would surge forward, waving money in their outstretched hands. For the price of one dollar each, the bottles of Meriwether's Elixir quickly sold out.

In 1899, Weil decided to strike out on his own. He left Meriwether and hit the road to sell *Hearth and Home* and distribute his cheap spoons and eyeglasses. An accomplished actor, Weil could improvise his manner and his lines to suit nearly every situation. His easygoing, honest manner easily convinced skeptics that he was sincere. Although he made a steady profit, Weil soon tired of the endless, lonesome walking through the countryside. He returned to Chicago and to the racetracks, where he devised several new ways to separate gamblers from their money.

Weil knew that most horse bettors were looking for a profitable bet on a "fixed" race (a race in which the horse owners agree on the winner beforehand). Posing as a horse expert, Weil would strike up conversations with any stranger who appeared to have money and good taste. Sooner or later, he would let drop some "inside information" on an upcoming race. Grateful for the advice, the gamblers readily agreed to extend a substantial loan, which Weil promised to repay from his own winnings.

Weil took his nickname, "Yellow Kid," from a character in the Hogan's Alley *comic strip.*

When the horse lost, as it usually did, Weil simply disappeared, several thousand dollars richer. Because they had illegally tried to profit from a fixed race, the gamblers could do nothing.

Weil made enough from these simple scams to set up his own "big store." The big store was a phony bookmaking establishment, where actors played the parts of cashiers, clerks, telegraph operators, and gamblers. The "gamblers" milled about the room, reading through the racing forms and talking over their chances. As race results came in over a telegraph wire, clerks posted the results on a chalkboard.

After selecting his "mark," or victim, Weil invited his new acquaintance to his establishment. He hooked him by promising to arrange an easy win. How could he do this? He needed the help of his brother-in-law, a telegraph operator at Western Union, who could temporarily hold back the race results. Before the results were wired to the clerks in the big store, the brother-in-law would use a complicated set of coded instructions to relay the result to Weil and the mark, who would then place their bets on the sure winner.

On the first try, however, the other "gamblers" always staged a loud commotion at the teller's cage. The pushing and shoving prevented the mark from putting down his bet. Frustrated, he could do nothing but listen to the results as his horse was announced the winner.

Determined not to miss out again, he would then put down even *more* money for the next race.

But this time, he lost.

Weil would shrug his shoulders and explain that, somehow, the mark had misunderstood the message from the brother-in-law.

After getting rid of his mark by staging a phony police "raid," Weil paid the actors for their time and counted out his profit. The big store was expensive to set up, but it brought in thousands of dollars every time it worked. Weil was beginning to live well indeed.

His victims could do nothing to recover their money because the law stated clearly that confidence games must "take unfair advantage of an unwary stranger" to be considered illegal. Weil had explained his operations in great detail and most of his marks were seeking to make their own illegal profit, so the law would never recognize them as "unwary strangers."

Hundreds of confidence men all over Chicago soon copied Weil's idea. But he eventually grew tired of his big-store operation and decided to invest in his own stable of horses instead. Weil set up his animals in expensive quarters and brought around wealthy gentlemen who wanted to turn a profit in a good race horse. He convinced them that, with a little training, his animals would easily win race after race.

Training, however, cost money, and Weil always claimed to be just a few thousand dollars short of what he needed to train his horses properly. His marks eagerly lent Weil the money he needed and then waited for their investments to pay off. They waited a long time because Weil made sure his horses never won any races. If they had won, of course, Weil would have had to repay the investment.

Weil pulled off dozens of these "ringer" deals, but the plan backfired after he hustled $2,500 from a Chicago woman named Madame Cleo. Determined to get back her money, Madame Cleo went to her boyfriend for help. Her boyfriend, a police detective, ordered Weil banned from the race track, and the swindler had to sell his horses.

But instead of going straight, Weil—perhaps the most imaginative confidence man ever to profit from the greedy and the gullible—simply moved from racing into a new field of operation: real estate.

To get started, he bought a large tract of inexpensive land in a remote area of Oceana County, in northern Michigan. Then, he rented a suite of offices in downtown Chicago, where he set up the Elysium Development Company. The business offices were well furnished and decorated with photographs of beautiful rolling lawns, lakes, hunting grounds, golf courses, tennis courts, and swimming pools.

Weil hired a close friend, Colonel Jim Porter, to work at his new company. A vivid and convincing story-teller, Colonel Porter had a very important connection in northern Michigan: his cousin was Oceana County's clerk of records.

Weil rounded up several hundred acquaintances and offered them free vacation lots in Michigan. Colonel Porter welcomed the clients into Elysium's offices, pointed out their lots on a map, and described the many pleasant vacations that awaited them in northern Michigan.

Delighted by their good fortune, the new landowners quickly agreed to the necessary legal details. They

Weil talks to reporters about one of his scams.

first had to record their lots with the county clerk, who would prepare the necessary paperwork for $15. The clerk also advised them to make sure the title to the land was clear by having an abstract (a record of the land's previous owners) made out for another $25. The many procedures became somewhat expensive for the clients. Weil would split the fees with Colonel Porter and Porter's cousin.

The three men roped in hundreds of customers and made a great deal of money. The clerk officially recorded the lots, and the titles were clear. Weil's customers were happy as long as they didn't bother to actually visit their free lots, which were located in a stretch of worthless, barren swampland far from any lake or tennis court.

Eventually, Weil and Porter succeeded in selling nearly all the lots they had bought in Oceana County. Although Weil retired from the business, Colonel Porter stayed on as a real estate salesman.

After closing up the Elysium Development Company, Weil turned to the most profitable swindle of his life: the stock market. With several partners, he invented the "boiler room," in which a group of salesmen worked in an office filled with telephones. Weil's "stock advisory service" contacted wealthy professionals—such as doctors and lawyers—and offered free advice on the market. At first, the salesmen sold legitimate stocks of well-known corporations. Later, they would call with a hot tip on a little-known and inexpensive stock that promised a

Weil talks his way out of court after being picked up
by a police sergeant who recognized the "Yellow Kid."

big return. Eager to make a profit, most victims agreed to switch out of their legitimate stocks.

To give his business a good front, Weil hired a market expert to write a newsletter. The newsletter always promoted the cheap stocks that Weil's salesmen were pushing in their phone calls. Many of these stocks were shares of obscure or bankrupt mining companies. Within a few months, the shares lost their value, and Weil and his partners kept most of their clients' money.

Although Weil later had to close up his "boiler room," the concept survived. Swindlers are still using telephone banks to sell low-priced stocks, worthless land, and phony bargain vacations. If the police close in, boiler-room operators can quickly abandon their offices, move to a safer place, and invent a new company name and a new sales pitch. Today, legitimate businesses also use "tele-marketers" to sell their products. It all began with Joseph Weil.

Although he was a skilled and creative con man, Weil occasionally tried to succeed at a legitimate business. He had a bad reputation in the Chicago area, however, so he invented a new name for himself: Richard E. Dorian. As Dorian, he formed a partnership with the owner of a coffee plantation (who didn't know his real identity) and devised "premium coupons," a new method for selling the product. One coupon came with each can of coffee. After collecting 150 coupons, Mr. Dorian's customers would be entitled to a gift: an upright piano.

Weil bought a large stock of cheap pianos for $45 each. He planned to sell his three-pound coffee cans for $1 (although the coffee would actually cost him less than 1¢ per pound). The customers would be paying $150 for 450 pounds of coffee and a piano. After expenses, "Dorian" and his partners would take in about $100 for each paid up, piano-playing coffee customer.

The business was set up in a Chicago warehouse that Weil and his partner fitted out with offices, a processing plant, and a showroom. The men succeeded in leasing the plant with no money down and quickly readied the business for operation.

Just as Weil was ready for the first day of his first legitimate business, an old friend showed up at the office. "Mr. Dorian" was out, so the man sat down to wait. Growing impatient, he pulled a set of dice from his pocket and proceeded to win a few dollars from Weil's partner. They argued, and Weil's true identity was revealed by his friend.

Surprised, Weil's new partner quickly backed out of the deal. He knew of Weil's reputation as a swindler and had no intention of being tricked. The business closed down immediately, and Weil never sold a single can of coffee or gave away one cheap piano. But Weil's "premium coupons" became a popular selling tool. Many large companies borrowed the idea, and coupons are now offered by cigarette companies and other businesses that know that everyone wants something for nothing.

Weil's fortunes improved with the coming of World War I. Britain and France were fighting the armies of Germany in western Europe. At first, the United States stayed out of the conflict. Later, America declared war on Germany and sent an expeditionary force to Europe. At the same time, Weil was finding out that, for many people, money was more important than patriotism.

Weil and his new partner, Fred "Deacon" Buckminster, posed as two German businessmen who wanted to purchase a factory for the production of war materials. Traveling to Indianapolis, the pair introduced themselves to a bank president who was a prominent citizen and the owner of a decrepit, empty factory. Weil offered a high price for the plant, and the bank president eagerly agreed to sell.

After they concluded the deal, Weil explained to the bank president that he had to wait for his superiors in Berlin to approve the deal. (This "stall" was an important part of many of Weil's confidence games. It made the mark even more eager to turn over money.) In the meantime, Weil mentioned that he owned a large block of stock in a little-known but very profitable mine. Weil's diversion of the impatient victim's attention to a different and even more tempting opportunity was the "switch."

Curious, the bank president asked for a chance to purchase some shares in the company. When Weil put him off, the banker's demands grew louder. Finally, Weil and his partner gave in and allowed the man to invest $50,000.

Leaving the bank president and his factory behind, Weil and Buckminster quickly left town with the money. But unlike many of Weil's victims, the Indianapolis banker went to the police. Using the banker's detailed description of the two men, the police arrested Weil, who was tried and sentenced to 18 months in a state penitentiary. (Although he would be out of circulation for a while, Weil never missed a chance to use his great talents. On his way to jail, he sold $30 worth of mining stock to one of the police detectives who was accompanying him.)

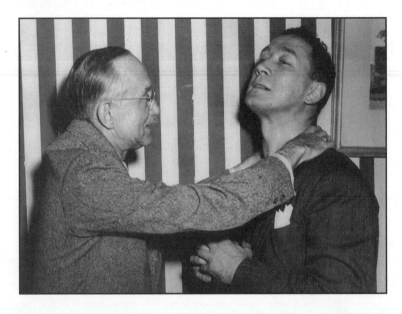

Weil demonstrates a choke hold on judo expert Ewald Biczek at a 1946 dinner for mystery writers.

After leaving prison, Weil decided to pursue no more swindles in Chicago. Instead, he would use the city only as a refuge. Determined to make money legally, he bought a hotel on Chicago's North Side. He named it the Hotel Martinique and added a restaurant, a laundry, and other facilities. For the convenience of his guests, he bought a large stock of liquor, which he provided to private parties.

Weil prepared to settle down to a comfortable and legal career as a hotel manager, but the Martinique soon faced a problem: It seemed that every swindler, gambler, and thief in Chicago was taking up residence there. The new tenants held noisy parties, wrote bad checks, and raided the hotel's liquor supply. Weil quickly began to lose money.

To meet his expenses, Weil was forced to sell most of his other property in Chicago. Desperate for money, he agreed to accept stolen bonds and stocks, which he then sold to raise cash. When the police finally raided the Martinique, they discovered the stolen bonds in Weil's room. The police arrested him, and Weil was sent to the federal prison in Leavenworth, Kansas.

Weil had made an important discovery: Con men almost always lose money when they try to make a legal business investment. Because swindlers love to spend lavishly on expensive luxuries, most simply don't have the discipline needed to run a legal business.

When Weil finally got out of Leavenworth in the late 1930s, war clouds were again gathering in Europe.

*Even slippery Joseph Weil couldn't escape from
Kansas's Leavenworth Penitentiary, which held him
for several years.*

Wars were always good opportunities for Weil. This
time, he devised a new con using one of his many false
identities: Dr. Henri Reuel, a distinguished mining engi-
neer. Dr. Reuel spoke with a slight accent and always
mentioned his important connections in Europe.

When Dr. Reuel learned that a wealthy woman in
Chicago wanted to sell some mining property in Arizona,
he explained to her that Germany needed a new source of
copper for its war factories. Reuel convinced her that he
could evaluate mining properties, and she agreed to hire
him.

Weil then made a leisurely trip to the Southwest,
which was paid for by his client, who also provided him

with a generous expense account. When he returned to Chicago, he suggested to the woman that a trip to Germany was necessary so that he could negotiate directly with Adolf Hitler. The woman agreed, and Weil headed to Europe.

Arriving in Berlin, Weil made a request to meet with Hitler. When the Nazi government denied his request, on official stationery, Weil used the stationery to forge official letters from Hitler and from a German bank. The letters indicated that the Germans were interested in buying the Arizona property.

Weil returned to Chicago and explained that negotiations had been delayed. But when the woman insisted that he return to Europe for another meeting with the German government, Dr. Reuel refused. Weil could sense that a war was coming, and he had no intention of being caught in Europe at the wrong time. When the woman cut off his expense account, Weil abandoned the scam and left town. In his haste, however, he failed to recover the documents forged on German stationery. He had violated one of the hustler's cardinal rules: Never leave incriminating evidence behind.

The woman complained, and the police were again on Weil's trail. He was arrested and convicted for the third time. While World War II consumed the nations of Europe, Weil was serving a peaceful jail term in Atlanta. Weil's stretch in Atlanta convinced him to go straight after his release in 1942. Weil took legitimate employment

Nazi leader Adolf Hitler (1889-1945) never met Joseph Weil, who was arrested for forging letters in the name of the German dictator.

after the war as a telephone solicitor. Using his easy and convincing manner, he raised money for charities, politicians, and church funds. His employers paid him a percentage of the money he raised, and Weil managed to make a comfortable living. He had managed to save little of the $8 million he had swindled over the years. He lived in a modest home and died in 1976.

Weil thought of his many successful hustles as more than illegal activities. He looked upon swindling as a way of teaching the rich a valuable lesson about their own greed. In each one of Weil's hustles, the mark had tried to get something for nothing—and ended up paying dearly.

Joseph Weil—one of the most successful con artists in history—testifies before the Senate Subcommittee on Juvenile Delinquency in 1956.

After being swindled himself, Iowa deputy sheriff Oscar Hartzell turned to a life of crime.

4

Oscar Hartzell
The Farmer Who Milked Millions

*T*he early twentieth century was a time of optimism in the United States. The country was one of the world's richest industrial powers. New inventions were making fortunes for businesses. Farmers were coaxing huge harvests from the fertile soil. Cities were growing, and settlers had conquered the western frontier.

Nevertheless, many people were poor and could only dream of a life of comfort and wealth. A common wish was to inherit a long-lost fortune; that millions of dollars would suddenly appear from the estate of a forgotten wealthy ancestor, and work and cares would be left behind.

Wherever people seek an easy way to riches, hoaxers will appear and try to sell them a way to make their dream come true. In the small towns of the Midwest, Sudie B. Whiteaker and Milo Lewis were spreading the rumor of just such a fortune: the gigantic estate of the long-dead English sea captain Sir Francis Drake.

Whiteaker and Lewis traveled to Iowa to find partners in their quest for the Drake estate. The Englishman had died centuries ago, they explained, and had left behind a hoard of gold treasure that added up to wealth beyond imagining. The Drake heirs were still alive, and many Drakes living right there in Iowa were legally entitled to part of the estate.

There were problems, however. For their own selfish reasons, the lawyers and officials in England who knew about the Drake inheritance wanted to keep it a secret. Some day soon, Whiteaker and Lewis would succeed in bringing the treasure back to its rightful heirs in the United States. Meanwhile, they needed partners. For a small fee that would be returned a hundred—perhaps a thousand—times over, they would obtain a fair share for anyone who wanted to participate.

On their travels in Iowa, the two hustlers visited the Hartzell farm in Madison County. Although the Hartzells were just getting by on the earnings from their crops and livestock, they believed the story of the Drake

British admiral Sir Francis Drake (1540?-1596) pirated hoards of treasure during his infamous career.

estate and turned over $6,000 of their savings. In return, Whiteaker and Lewis promised to include the family when the English courts finally settled the estate.

The story of the Drake inheritance was indeed bringing in a lot of money, but Whiteaker and Lewis never returned to the Hartzell farm. Like hundreds of other hopeful families throughout the Midwest, the Hartzells were left poorer, sadder, and wiser. Unlike most people who were swindled, however, Oscar Hartzell soon realized what had happened to his family. He set off to find Whiteaker and Lewis.

As a deputy sheriff, Oscar Hartzell made use of his contacts in law enforcement to track down Whiteaker and Lewis in Des Moines, the Iowa capital. He questioned the pair and discovered that they had collected $65,000 in just two months. But Hartzell had no intention of making an arrest or of claiming his family's money. Instead, he established the Sir Francis Drake Association and made the Drake inheritance his own.

The three confidence artists joined forces to collect investors for the Drake inheritance in Iowa, Missouri, and Illinois. They went house to house, called on businesses, and held open meetings. At first, they contacted only people with the last name Drake. Of course, family names can change after nearly 350 years, so Hartzell later decided to accept any and all families who might claim to be Drake heirs.

Hartzell eventually appointed himself manager and organizer of the scheme. He hired several aides and sales agents to work for him. The team signed up hundreds of families, occasionally enlisting entire towns to join the cause. As the money began to come in regularly, Hartzell began paying himself a salary of $1,000 every week.

In 1924, Hartzell decided to leave for England, where, he claimed, he could closely watch the progress of the Drake inheritance case. After arriving in London, he wrote back to the association to say that he had met the real Drake heir, who was willing to share the fortune with his partners back in the United States. The two men would cooperate in pursuing the case through the English courts.

Hartzell reported that their task would be difficult and that it might take years and cost millions of dollars in legal fees. To win the case, he said, he would need further contributions from all those who already had joined in the Drake inheritance. If he succeeded, he promised to repay all investments at the rate of 500 to 1.

Hartzell's sales agents, who themselves had bought into the scheme, made large contributions of their own. Even the swindlers were being swindled! Because the agents believed in the scheme, they had no trouble convincing thousands of people that, thanks to the efforts of Oscar Hartzell, the Drake fortune would soon be theirs.

While his investors back in the United States were turning their savings over to his sales agents, Hartzell was living well in London. He bought fine clothes and stayed in a luxurious suite of rooms in one of the city's best neighborhoods. He rode in chauffeured limousines to London's finest restaurants and clubs. He even adopted a noble British title: the Duke of Buckland.

To keep up appearances, the duke needed a constant flow of cash, so he ordered his agents to send him more money—$2,500 each week. The agents forwarded the money to his brother, Canfield, who had opened an office in Toronto. Canfield then sent the money to Oscar in the form of American Express money orders. (Oscar knew

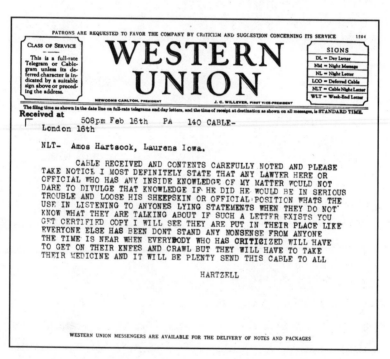

PATRONS ARE REQUESTED TO FAVOR THE COMPANY BY CRITICISM AND SUGGESTION CONCERNING ITS SERVICE   1204

CLASS OF SERVICE		SIGNS
This is a full-rate Telegram or Cablegram unless its deferred character is indicated by a suitable sign above or preceding the address.	**WESTERN UNION**	DL = Day Letter
		NM = Night Message
		NL = Night Letter
		LCO = Deferred Cable
		NLT = Cable Night Letter
		WLT = Week-End Letter

NEWCOMB CARLTON, PRESIDENT   J. C. WILLEVER, FIRST VICE-PRESIDENT

The filing time as shown in the date line on full-rate telegrams and day letters, and the time of receipt at destination as shown on all messages, is STANDARD TIME.

Received at
508pm Feb 16th   PA   140 CABLE-
London 16th

NLT- Amos Hartsock, Laurens Iowa.

        CABLE RECEIVED AND CONTENTS CAREFULLY NOTED AND PLEASE
TAKE NOTICE I MOST DEFINITELY STATE THAT ANY LAWYER HERE OR
OFFICIAL WHO HAS ANY INSIDE KNOWLEDGE OF MY MATTER WOULD NOT
DARE TO DIVULGE THAT KNOWLEDGE IF HE DID HE WOULD BE IN SERIOUS
TROUBLE AND LOOSE HIS SHEEPSKIN OR OFFICIAL POSITION WHATS THE
USE IN LISTENING TO ANYONES LYING STATEMENTS WHEN THEY DO NOT
KNOW WHAT THEY ARE TALKING ABOUT IF SUCH A LETTER EXISTS YOU
GET CERTIFIED COPY I WILL SEE THEY ARE PUT IN THEIR PLACE LIKE
EVERYONE ELSE HAS BEEN DONT STAND ANY NONSENSE FROM ANYONE
THE TIME IS NEAR WHEN EVERYBODY WHO HAS CRITICIZED WILL HAVE
TO GET ON THEIR KNEES AND CRAWL BUT THEY WILL HAVE TO TAKE
THEIR MEDICINE AND IT WILL BE PLENTY SEND THIS CABLE TO ALL

                        HARTZELL

WESTERN UNION MESSENGERS ARE AVAILABLE FOR THE DELIVERY OF NOTES AND PACKAGES

Oscar Hartzell used telegrams to conduct his business correspondence.

that the U.S. law prohibited collecting money through the mail for fraudulent schemes.)

At one point, high living got Oscar Hartzell into serious trouble. While he was carrying on a love affair with a young English woman, the woman became pregnant. Her father called on Hartzell and angrily demanded that a marriage take place as soon as possible.

Hartzell managed to calm the man and explain the situation. He was working on an important case that would reward him and all of his clients in the United States with an immense fortune. With the many claims on his time and energy, he could never give a wife the attention she deserved. As soon as the case was resolved, however, he would be happy to marry her.

In the meantime, he had an excellent idea that would solve any financial worries the man or his daughter might have. Perhaps they would be interested in making a contribution of their own? The family was not related to Sir Francis Drake, but as a favor Hartzell offered to accept them as official Drake heirs at the price of 500 English pounds (worth $2125 in the United States). The man accepted immediately, and Oscar quickly broke off relations with the young woman.

As the years dragged on and Canfield's money orders continued to arrive, Oscar's claims became more grandiose. In a top-secret letter to be read to the Drake heirs at one of the association's regular meetings, he announced that the value of the estate was much larger

Oscar Hartzell issued receipts to people who contributed to the bogus Sir Francis Drake Association, which collected more than $2 million.

than he had thought. In fact, with all the money that was about to be released, he could buy the entire state of Iowa and put a fence around it!

Yet he maintained that problems continued to plague his work in England: The English courts would not recognize his claims, the English government was against him, and the English king was watching over the case and stood ready to block any settlement. Indeed, Hartzell claimed, the financial system of the entire world was determined to stop him.

Hartzell also announced that he and the real Drake heir were having long and serious discussions. They both realized the case could drag on forever. Because legal fees and other costs were so high, the Drake heir had decided to accept contributions from anyone, even those who would have no claim whatsoever on the estate.

As the case dragged on, the first murmurs and complaints were reaching Hartzell. To calm his nervous investors, Hartzell began sending cables announcing a settlement. The English government was preparing to release the fortune soon, he said, and only a few delays and legal problems remained. His reassurance caused the flow of money to resume at an even greater pace.

Hartzell now began to blame international conspiracies for the long wait: The stock market crash of 1929 was deliberately caused by governments attempting to stop the Drake settlement, and the Great Depression was another worldwide conspiracy. Hartzell also accused his followers of hurting his efforts through their own loose tongues. He warned that any breach of secrecy in the United States would set back his efforts and that anyone who talked to the press or the police could spoil the entire enterprise.

Despite Hartzell's warnings, details of the scheme were leaking out, and the U.S. government began to investigate. The federal authorities had a problem, however. The hopeful Drake heirs were unwilling to file complaints because Hartzell's agents had sworn them to absolute secrecy. One word to the authorities and their claim to the Drake treasure would disappear as quickly as a desert mirage.

By the early 1930s, Hartzell and his agents had recruited 70,000 people to become heirs of Sir Francis Drake. New investors were selling their homes and land in order to raise money and sign up with Hartzell. The entire scheme had now taken in more than $2 million. At their secret meetings, the agents announced that billions of dollars would soon be transferred from England to the United States. To heighten the suspense, Hartzell reported that he had rejected a low settlement offer from the English government.

In 1932, as some of his subscribers began questioning the entire scheme, Hartzell told his followers that a final date had been set for a settlement. By this time, however, the authorities were catching up to Hartzell's agents in the Midwest, and several of them were arrested on the charge of fraud. The U.S. State Department asked for Hartzell's extradition from England. The English government gladly complied. In January 1933, Oscar Hartzell's life as the Duke of Buckland came to an end. With several police agents accompanying him, he boarded a ship for the United States, where a criminal trial awaited him.

Hartzell wouldn't surrender without a fight. He told his followers to write their representatives in the United States Congress to demand an end to the investigation. Thousands did so, convinced that the government was conspiring to shut down Hartzell's operation and to cheat them out of their rightful inheritance.

After landing in the United States, Hartzell was arrested by U.S. federal agents, charged with mail fraud, and jailed in Sioux City, Iowa. Confident that he would

Even after Hartzell's arrest, many people still believed they would share the lost treasure of Sir Francis Drake.

eventually go free, he convinced many of his investors that England would release the Drake inheritance as soon as the court declared him innocent. Hartzell easily raised a large sum for his legal defense.

In the meantime, English officials had unearthed the genuine will of Sir Francis Drake, and a team of legal experts traveled to Sioux City to give their evidence at Hartzell's trial. According to the experts, there were no Drake children and no unknown heirs. Furthermore, their documents revealed that Drake's inheritance, which in fact amounted to very little, had gone to his widow and to one of his brothers.

Still, Hartzell's investors didn't lose faith, and lawyers for the defense found many of them who were willing to testify in Hartzell's behalf. Yet the government had a strong case against him. Although he had never used the mails himself to work the scam, he had "caused others" to do so, which made him guilty of mail fraud. The court convicted Hartzell and gave him a ten-year sentence.

In November 1933, Oscar Hartzell arrived at the gates of Leavenworth Penitentiary in Kansas to begin his sentence. Convinced he was the victim of a diabolical international conspiracy, Hartzell gradually went out of his mind. The government later transferred him to a federal medical facility in Springfield, Missouri, where he died before completing his sentence.

The Duke of Buckland was behind bars, and the country was in the middle of the Great Depression. Unemployment and poverty were widespread, factories had shut down, and farms were going bankrupt. Yet many people still believed in their dreams. Despite Hartzell's trial and his long prison sentence, the Sir Francis Drake Association continued to receive contributions. Oscar Hartzell may have been a fraud, but he gave many people hope during difficult times.

A nationally known performer and prankster by his mid-twenties, Orson Welles (1915-85) never duplicated the level of success he had achieved early in his career.

5

Orson Welles
The Accidental Hoax

On a dark Sunday evening in the autumn of 1938, millions of families tuned in to the CBS Mercury Theatre, starring Orson Welles. Gathered around their radios, they listened to a deep, resonant voice that held them spellbound.

We know now that in the early years of the twentieth century this world was being watched closely by intelligences greater than man's.

For six months, Welles, his producer, John Houseman, and writer Howard Koch had adapted novels, plays, and stories for the radio. The three men worked hard to make their shows as realistic as possible. Every Sunday night, Welles's dramatic presentations drew his audience into a convincing world of drama and suspense.

The broadcast of October 30, 1938, began at 8:00 P.M. Eastern time. But instead of a radio play, listeners heard soft music and a soothing voice.

Good evening, ladies and gentlemen. From the Meridian Room in the Park Plaza in New York City, we bring you the music of Ramon Raquello and his orchestra.

A week beforehand, John Houseman called Howard Koch to give the writer his next project: adapting a short novel entitled *The War of the Worlds* by the English novelist H. G. Wells. Koch had to describe an invasion of Earth by aliens from Mars. Orson Welles, who would play the part of a scientist in the show, thought "The War of the Worlds" would make for an amusing and harmless story.

Koch had a tough assignment and very little time. *The War of the Worlds* was set in England, so for the sake of realism, he would need to invent new characters, move the scene to the United States, and change the prose descriptions of the book into dialogue for radio. In just six days, he had to write an almost entirely original script. He called Houseman back to ask for more time, but the

Science-fiction writer H.G. Wells wrote The War of the Worlds, *but he knew nothing about Orson Welles's plan to adapt the book for radio.*

answer was no. Welles wanted "The War of the Worlds" for the next performance—just in time for Halloween.

Koch had one important advantage: He was working in a medium that forces the audience to use its imagination. To help his own imagination along, the writer picked up a road map of the state of New Jersey. He would set his story in a rural area, which would become the landing point for the first Martian spacecraft. Blindly letting his pencil fall in the middle of the map, he selected Grovers Mill, a small town near Princeton.

Ladies and gentlemen, we interrupt our program of dance music to bring you a special news bulletin from the Intercontinental Radio News. At twenty minutes before eight, central time, Professor Farrell of the Mount Jennings Observatory, Chicago, Illinois, reports observing several explosions of incandescent gas occurring at regular intervals on the planet Mars.

The broadcast had begun; the sweet strains of string music were pleasant and familiar. Yet lurking in the background were troubling events on the planet Mars. From time to time, a stern announcer interrupted the broadcast, using a voice heavy with foreboding. He reported more gas explosions on Mars and the sighting of unknown objects hurtling at high speed toward Earth.

Koch knew that the town of Princeton, near Grovers Mill, was the site of a prestigious university. He

Orson Welles reads a radio script from the Columbia Broadcasting Building during the late 1930s.

created a fictitious Princeton scientist, Professor Richard Pierson, to report on the mysterious events. The audience might not believe reporters and news bulletins, but they would certainly believe a scientist.

We are ready now to take you to the Princeton Observatory at Princeton where Carl Phillips, our commentator, will interview Professor Richard Pierson, famous astronomer. We take you now to Princeton, New Jersey.

The interview began. In a calm voice, Professor Pierson explained that, as far as he and all other astronomers knew, no life existed on Mars. He had no explanation for the explosions seen on that planet.

Suddenly, the announcer broke into the interview. A meteorite had fallen in New Jersey. Within seconds, a reporter had arrived on the scene—a remote farmer's field near Grovers Mill. The reporter reached the point of impact and spoke calmly:

I guess that's it. Yes, I guess that's the . . . thing, directly in front of me, half buried in a vast pit. It looks more like a huge cylinder. . . . The color is sort of yellowish white.

The CBS radio network had announced at the beginning of the broadcast that the Mercury Theatre was about to present a play based on a work of fiction by H. G. Wells. But most people paid no attention to commercials and announcements. They began to listen only when the show began. Later, while the program was underway, many more listeners switched over to the Mercury Theatre from other stations. Listening intently, the growing audience began to feel a rising surge of fear.

. . . it's becoming more distinct. Perhaps you've caught it already on your radio. Listen: Do you hear it? It's a curious humming sound that seems to come from inside the object. . . . Just a minute! Something's happening! Ladies and gentlemen, this is terrific! . . . The top is beginning to rotate like a screw! The thing must be hollow!

The voice of the announcer began to lose its steady calm. Screams of terror could be heard in the background. There was confusion and panic at Grovers Mill. On the Mercury Theatre broadcast, the music had stopped.

Someone's crawling out of the hollow top. Someone or . . . something. . . . Something's wiggling out of the shadow like a gray snake. It's large as a bear, and it glistens like wet leather. But that face. It . . . it's indescribable.

It was about 8:15 P.M. when the first telephone calls began flooding the switchboards at police stations and newspapers. People were running out of their homes and apartments to search the nighttime sky. At the

By 1938, astronomers had concluded there was no life on Mars, but thousands of Americans listening to "The War of the Worlds" weren't so sure.

Columbia Broadcasting Building, Orson Welles was preparing his audience for the end of the world.

I can hardly force myself to keep looking at it. The eyes are black and gleam like a serpent. The mouth is V-shaped with saliva dripping from its rimless lips that seem to quiver and pulsate.

Within a few minutes, traffic jammed the roads leading out of New York City. The police were taking thousands of emergency calls. Some listeners fainted at the foot of their radio consoles, while others went into shock. A woman in Pittsburgh was preparing to end her life with a bottle of poison.

A humped shape is rising out of the pit. I can make out a small beam of light against a mirror. What's that? There's a jet of flame springing from that mirror, and it leaps right at the advancing men. It strikes them head on! Good Lord, they're turning into flame!

The broadcast pulled in millions of additional listeners as word of the invasion spread. Howard Koch had succeeded too well in making his script convincing. At first, the program offered a typical musical broadcast. Then, short news bulletins—confusing at first, then alarming, and then terrifying—interrupted the music. Koch had used familiar places in the New Jersey

This book illustration from The War of the Worlds *shows the horrifying invasion that 1938 radio listeners thought was really taking place.*

countryside, and well-known roads, landmarks, and high-ways to add realism to the story. By inventing Professor Pierson, a trusted figure with knowledge and authority, the writer made the events even more believable.

As the invasion continued and Martian ships landed all over the eastern United States, higher authorities appealed to the nation for calm. An air force commander assured the audience that his planes would be able to turn back the invasion:

I have been requested by the governor of New Jersey to place the counties of Mercer and Middlesex . . . under martial law. . . . Four companies of state militia are proceeding from Trenton to Grovers Mill, and will aid in the evacuation of homes within the range of military operations.

Then, after a few moments, listeners heard the grave and steady voice of the Secretary of the Interior:

Citizens of the nation: I shall not try to conceal the gravity of the situation that confronts the country, nor the concern of your government in protecting the lives and property of its people. . . . Fortunately, this formidable enemy is still confined to a comparatively small area, and we may place our faith in the military forces to keep them there.

A battery of artillery fired deadly cannons against the Martian spacecraft—but with no effect. A dogfight between an air force squadron and the aliens ended as eight fighter planes and their pilots plunged helplessly from the skies. As the show continued, the listeners could hear plainly that the Martians were easily destroying the armed might of the United States. There was no way to stop them and nowhere to hide. Earth was doomed.

According to the broadcast, poisonous gas was pouring into the fields and marshes of New Jersey. Meanwhile, the Martian spacecraft were crossing the Hudson River into crowded Manhattan. Street by street, the aliens ravaged the city's skyscrapers with their precise and deadly heat rays. With no hope for their homes or families, crowds of people fled toward the East River and plunged into the cold, black waters to save themselves.

The end had come. Then, another announcement came from the top of the Columbia Broadcasting Building:

Our army wiped out . . . artillery, air force, everything wiped out. This may be the last broadcast. We'll stay here to the end. . . . People are holding service below us . . . in the cathedral.

After a commercial break and more announcements, Professor Pierson came back on the air. He had met a stranger at a farmhouse near Grovers Mill, ground zero of the Martian invasion. Both men were taking refuge from the aliens. The last survivors of the invasion, they carried on an aimless conversation as the world burned around them.

At the very end, Orson Welles made a final announcement:

This is Orson Welles, ladies and gentlemen, out of character to assure you that The War of the Worlds has no further significance than as the holiday offering it was intended to be. . . . So goodbye, everybody, and remember, please, the terrible lesson you learned tonight. That grinning, glowing, globular invader of your living room is an inhabitant of the pumpkin patch, and if your doorbell rings and nobody's there, that was no Martian . . . it's Halloween.

Panic spread across the land as Welles finished his Halloween prank. A crowd of people quickly showed up at the Columbia Broadcasting studios, trapping Welles and Koch in their offices. Police officers occupied the studios and hallways of the building while network officials quickly locked up or destroyed all copies of the script. Meanwhile, the cast and crew escaped the building through a back door.

The next day, newspapers carried banner headlines describing the nationwide panic. Orson Welles and the Mercury Theatre had some explaining to do. Senator Clyde Herring proposed a censorship board to screen future radio broadcasts for harmful content. The Federal Communications Commission began an investigation.

Several listeners filed lawsuits, claiming to have suffered damage as a result of the broadcast.

"The War of the Worlds" broadcast was the start of an impressive career for Orson Welles. Famous as the radio announcer who had terrified the nation, Welles was welcomed in Hollywood, where he was given complete control over his first motion picture, the highly successful *Citizen Kane*. Howard Koch also found his way to the

At age 25, Orson Welles wrote, directed, and starred in the 1941 classic, Citizen Kane, *which many critics now consider the greatest motion picture ever made.*

movie industry, where the work was easier and the pay much better. One of his first writing projects was to collect a few fragments of dialogue and description and turn them into a movie script. The result was the 1942 picture *Casablanca*, which became a Hollywood classic.

After the panic had died down, public opinion turned favorable. Radio listeners were able to laugh at the prank. Orson Welles said only, "It was our thought that perhaps people might be bored or annoyed at hearing a tale so improbable."

At Grovers Mill, however, the invasion had just begun. Tourists came from all over the country to visit the site of the Martian landing, a site that Orson Welles, Howard Koch and John Houseman had never seen. Within a year, the outbreak of World War II made people forget "The War of the Worlds." Instead, for the next six years, radio bulletins would be describing a harsh reality—a real war and real invasions on planet Earth.

Although Clifford Irving continued to work as a writer, his reputation was forever tarnished by his 1971 plan to write a fake autobiography of Howard Hughes.

6

Clifford Irving
The Writer Who Faked History

*C*lifford Irving enjoyed the good life. A successful writer with several novels to his credit, he lived on the sunny Mediterranean island of Ibiza, where he owned a comfortable house and 15 acres of land. His books had earned him plenty of money, and the McGraw-Hill publishing company was eager to offer him a generous contract for another book.

Early in the 1970s, however, Irving began to suffer uncomfortable doubts. Perhaps his life had become *too* easy. Ibiza offered little adventure, and writing novels no longer posed much of a challenge for him. Instead of working on his books, Irving spent his time going to parties. Though his novels were selling well enough, he had never enjoyed the riches and fame that came with a big best-seller. Was he just wasting his talents and his time?

To cure his restlessness, Irving dreamed up one of the most elaborate hoaxes in history. It would be difficult to carry off, but it would seal his fate. He would either retire as a famous and wealthy man, or he would bring his writing career to a spectacular end. It would all depend on his publisher—and on a very mysterious tycoon.

With a long list of fiction and nonfiction titles, McGraw-Hill was one of the biggest and richest book companies in the world. Its directors and managers never forgot that they were in business to make money—preferably much more money than their competitors.

In early 1971, McGraw-Hill showed a keen interest when Clifford Irving reported that he had contacted Howard Hughes, a famous but very secretive billionaire. Hughes had enjoyed reading one of Irving's novels, and the two men were now carrying on a friendly correspondence. In fact, for the first time in 15 years, Howard Hughes might grant an interview—to Clifford Irving.

Such an interview—even better, a full-length autobiography by Hughes himself—would be worth millions to any publisher. Hughes was a fascinating figure who had already been the subject of several books and hundreds of news stories. The owner of the Hughes Aircraft

*Billionaire Howard Hughes (1905-1976) had gained
international attention as a young man—and
Hughes's reclusive nature kept the public continually
interested in him.*

Corporation, he had made a fortune on government contracts for defense goods. He had produced movies, bought hotels, and designed the *Spruce Goose*, one of the largest airplanes ever built.

Despite his fame and money, Hughes lived like a fugitive. He stayed alone in secret hotel rooms and employed aides and bodyguards to keep reporters away. He never gave out information about himself. Several publishers had already offered him book contracts, but he had expressed no interest. He wanted, above all, to be left alone.

The Hughes HK-1 Hercules—*also known as the* Spruce Goose—*had eight engines and could carry up to 700 soldiers.*

After McGraw-Hill heard from Clifford Irving, the company asked him to drop the novel he was working on and contact Hughes immediately. Irving and Richard Suskind, a close friend, began to research their Hughes "autobiography." The two men would pretend to hold secret, taped interviews with Hughes. They would then send transcripts of the phony interviews to Irving's editor. If McGraw-Hill accepted the interviews as genuine, Irving would rewrite the tapes and create the first and only autobiography of Howard Hughes.

How could the hoax work when Hughes was still alive? Wouldn't he deny that Irving had interviewed him? Irving was counting on Hughes's own fanatic demand for privacy. The billionaire never appeared in public and never talked to the press. If the book came out, Hughes would have to come out in the open in order to claim it was a fake. Irving believed that Hughes would never do this. And neither McGraw-Hill nor the public would know if the book were true or not. With a little luck and care, Irving would fool everyone and get rich as well.

In February, Irving flew to New York with some letters that Hughes had supposedly written to him. In these letters, "Hughes" claimed that he simply wanted to tell the truth about his life. He would use the book to put all the rumors to rest and reveal himself to the world. Irving had spent several days carefully forging Hughes's distinctive handwriting. Eager for a publishing sensation, McGraw-Hill's executives accepted the letters as genuine.

The company then made an offer for the book. Hughes would be paid a total of $500,000 in three installments. He would receive $100,000 after signing the contract, $100,000 after McGraw-Hill accepted the interviews, and $300,000 when the publisher accepted the manuscript of the book.

Irving reported that Hughes accepted the offer with one important condition: All communication must be through Clifford Irving, who would also be the only one allowed to handle McGraw-Hill's payments. Certain that they had a best-seller, McGraw-Hill's executives accepted the condition. Hoping to keep the book a complete secret before publication, the company gave Hughes the code name "Octavio." At the offices of McGraw-Hill, Irving's book became known as "Project Octavio."

After returning to Ibiza, Irving typed up an agreement, signed Hughes's name at the bottom, and sent the document to McGraw-Hill. The company's lawyers carefully examined the contract and pronounced the signature and the contract to be genuine.

Nevertheless, several executives at McGraw-Hill were beginning to have doubts about Project Octavio. Despite all the money the company would be paying, none of them had yet spoken to Hughes or to any of his many lawyers and aides. On the other hand, Irving seemed to be gaining very little for all his time and work. Hughes would get most of the money, and Irving would receive a large profit through royalties only if the book became a best-seller.

The company overruled its doubters and made out a check to Irving, who then had a bank split the money into two checks: one for Irving and one for "H. R. Hughes." (Irving claimed that Hughes insisted on this spelling.)

One important problem remained: how to cash the Hughes check. Irving quickly came up with another plan. He created a fake passport for his wife, Edith, in the name of "Helga Hughes." Edith traveled to Switzerland to open a bank account as "H. R. Hughes." She deposited McGraw-Hill's check and then used a disguise and a second set of false identity papers to open an account in another bank. Edith withdrew the money from the "H. R. Hughes" account, placed it in the second account, and then withdrew most of this deposit.

Irving had turned $10,000 over to Richard Suskind before Edith's trip to Switzerland. The two men decided to invest their money rather than spend it. If McGraw-Hill discovered the hoax, Irving and Suskind would return the money. If McGraw-Hill published the book and Howard Hughes kept silent, they would collect royalties, as well as Hughes's contract fees, and live out their lives as the richest men on Ibiza.

Irving and Suskind now faced their most important task: research. In order to make the interviews with Hughes believable, they had to learn all they could about

Clifford Irving may have been the mastermind behind the "Hughes" deception, but the Swiss government was more interested in his wife, Edith—alias Helga Hughes.

the secretive billionaire and his past. In April 1971, the two men began a long and exhausting trip through the United States. They flew to Las Vegas, where Hughes owned a share of several hotels, and to Houston, where Hughes had spent his childhood. They read newspapers, examined documents, and interviewed Hughes's friends and colleagues.

In Los Angeles, Irving and Suskind spoke to aircraft executives and movie producers. At the Library of Congress in Washington, D.C., Irving examined testimony that Hughes had given to the United States Senate during an investigation in 1947. Hughes's statements had been taken down word for word and filled hundreds of pages. The testimony would help Irving and Suskind fake hours of recorded interviews.

Finally, Irving arrived in New York, where *Life* magazine kept a top secret file on Hughes. *Life* cooperated with Irving because the magazine had bought the rights to publish excerpts from the book. While searching through the files, Irving discovered thousands of pages of unpublished facts and details. Although *Life* had featured many articles about Hughes in the past, the magazine had not used most of this information.

With these details, Irving could easily fool the public and his editors into believing he had gained Hughes's confidence. He copied all the files he could use. The excerpts bought by *Life* magazine from Project Octavio would carry *Life's* own information—carefully disguised and rearranged by Irving and Suskind.

The research trip proved to be a great success. But in May, trouble appeared. In Los Angeles, Irving had called on Stanley Meyer, a Hollywood producer. Meyer told Irving that Noah Dietrich, an old associate of Howard Hughes, was preparing a book about Hughes. In fact, Meyer had the manuscript right there in his house. Dietrich had used a ghostwriter for the book, but it was in poor shape. Meyer then asked Irving to rewrite the Dietrich manuscript.

Noah Dietrich's manuscript was sheer coincidence. If it were published, however, it might cast suspicion on Irving's own project. The two books might disagree on facts, dates, names, and places. Irving agreed to look at the manuscript, which he secretly photocopied.

Irving discovered that Noah Dietrich had a wealth of information on Hughes that only a close associate could know. Dietrich had described informal conversations and had written about the billionaire's business methods in great detail. But the two men had become enemies, and Dietrich had taken revenge by filling his book with unflattering details about Hughes. Irving turned down Meyer's offer and gave back Dietrich's original manuscript—but he kept the photocopy. He planned to incorporate much of Dietrich's information into his own work.

Former Hughes employee Noah Dietrich tried to write an authentic biography of the billionaire, but the poor quality of the manuscript prevented it from being published.

Their notebooks crammed with facts, Suskind and Irving returned to Ibiza and set to work on the "interviews" with Hughes. The two writers locked themselves into a private study, where they set up a typewriter, a microphone, and a tape recorder. Irving and Suskind took turns pretending to be Hughes while the other conducted the interview. They imagined questions, answers, and dozens of stories, adding details as well as elaborate—and usually false—descriptions. The two men recounted Hughes's childhood in Texas, his business ventures in California, his career as a movie producer, and his work as a defense contractor. "Hughes" told fascinating tales of a journey to India to meet a renowned guru and a stay in Cuba with the writer Ernest Hemingway.

The two men recorded 20 hours of interviews and then typed them into 950 pages of transcript. When they were finished, Irving and Suskind burned the tapes, the copies of the *Life* magazine files, and the photocopy of Noah Dietrich's manuscript. They then sent the transcripts to New York. McGraw-Hill's editors and executives carefully read through the interviews, checking as many facts as they could. When they finished, they were unanimously convinced that the interviews were genuine.

Project Octavio was working according to plan. Irving decided to take full advantage of the situation by faking a note from Hughes to McGraw-Hill. In the note, Hughes raised his demands: He now wanted $850,000 for the book and an additional amount for the publication of excerpts by *Life*.

These new demands outraged McGraw-Hill's executives. But Project Octavio was too near completion to be allowed to slip away. Still convinced that they had a golden opportunity, they agreed to raise Hughes's total fee to $750,000. As they suspected all along, Howard Hughes was turning out to be a wily financial wizard who would do his best to outmaneuver them. McGraw-Hill made out another large check and turned it over to Irving. In late September, Edith Irving returned to Switzerland to deposit, transfer, and then withdraw the money from her two bank accounts.

As the project neared completion, another snag developed. McGraw-Hill began making plans to announce the book's official release. This worried Irving, who knew that an early announcement would cause controversy and perhaps even a denial from Hughes himself.

To solve the problem, Irving forged another note. Hughes now demanded that McGraw-Hill make its final payment *before* announcing the book's publication. The company agreed and turned over another $325,000. In December, Irving completed the book, wrote an introduction, and sent the manuscript to his publisher.

After accepting the manuscript, McGraw-Hill announced its forthcoming publication: *The Autobiography of Howard Hughes*. The subtitle read: *With Introduction and Commentary by Clifford Irving*.

The format of the book was unique. The interviews with Hughes were presented word for word, with no editing. Irving had added only his commentary and description. At a press meeting, the company announced that the book would be available in three months—in March 1972.

Immediately after the announcement, a spokesman from the Hughes Tool Company denounced the entire project. Nevertheless, McGraw-Hill forged ahead. The company had received offers of $325,000 from the Book of the Month Club, which would sell a special edition to its members, and Dell Books offered $400,000 for the right to publish a paperback version. With interest in the book running high, McGraw-Hill planned to print a first edition of 500,000 copies.

Howard Hughes quickly learned of the project. But instead of remaining quiet, as Irving and Suskind had hoped, the billionaire used a former acquaintance, Frank McCulloch, to issue a denial. In a telephone conversation with McCulloch—the last journalist to interview him—Hughes claimed that he had never heard of Clifford Irving. Furthermore, Hughes said, his own aides had discovered that money was being deposited in his name in a Swiss bank. Hughes promised to notify the Swiss police and sue McGraw-Hill and Clifford Irving if the company published the book.

Clifford Irving claimed that a Hughes imposter had fooled McCulloch. To back up Project Octavio,

*Clifford Irving fooled the McGraw-Hill publishing
company, but Howard Hughes (above) knew that
Irving's "autobiography" was a fake.*

117

McGraw-Hill turned the "Hughes" letters written by Irving over to a company that specialized in handwriting analysis. In a short time, the experts at Osborn, Osborn, and Osborn announced that the letters were genuine. Feeling confident, Irving boldly demanded that he be given a lie-detector test. McGraw-Hill agreed, but decided not to release the result of the test.

Hughes's conversation with Frank McCulloch was having an effect, however. Editors had discovered similarities between Irving's book and Noah Dietrich's manuscript. The Swiss police had begun an investigation of their own and had deduced that "H. R. Hughes" had been an imposter. Slowly at first, then more quickly, the hoax fell apart.

At first, Irving wasn't ready to admit failure. He claimed that one of Hughes's employees must have opened the accounts in Switzerland. But after searching bank records and questioning bank employees, the Swiss police fingered Irving's wife as the woman who had deposited and then withdrawn the checks made out to "H. R. Hughes." The Swiss then issued a warrant for the arrest of Edith Irving.

As soon as word of the Swiss warrant was released, the press began hounding the Irvings in Ibiza. A hot story was developing: the swindling of one of the world's largest publishers for three-quarters of a million dollars. Rumors of the gigantic hoax were flying in Europe as well as in the United States. To counter the reports,

Irving accepted an invitation from Mike Wallace to appear on "60 Minutes," a televised investigative show. Under sharp questioning by Wallace, Irving insisted that *The Autobiography of Howard Hughes* was real.

But later, when a New York district attorney announced that he would bring charges against Irving for fraud, the writer broke down and confessed. The hoax was finally over. The district attorney's investigation quickly turned up the true facts. Irving and Suskind decided to cooperate and plead guilty in hopes of receiving light sentences. Irving insisted, however, that his wife be protected from prosecution. Although the Swiss government promised U.S. authorities that they would spare Edith Irving a trial, they went back on their word as soon as information about the deal leaked to the press.

Clifford Irving had thought of his scheme as nothing more than a good prank. If no one had discovered the hoax, there would have been no problem. McGraw-Hill would have sold half a million books, *Life* magazine would have sold several million magazines, and Irving and Suskind would have become rich men. But Irving had counted on the silence of Howard Hughes. That had been his mistake.

The Swiss and U.S. governments were not amused by Irving's hoax. Clifford and Edith Irving and Richard Suskind pled guilty to fraud and received jail sentences. Irving spent 17 months in prison, and Suskind was jailed for 5 months. Edith Irving served 2 months in prison in

Clifford and Edith Irving dreamed of getting rich,
but instead they got time in prison.

the United States and then 14 months in a Swiss prison. An idle dream on the island of Ibiza had cost Clifford Irving his reputation and his freedom. Instead of riches, he gained only an honorary title from *Time* magazine as "Con Man of the Year."

Despite their sincere on-air appearance, television evangelists Tammy and Jim Bakker got rich by lying to their viewers.

7

Jim and Tammy Bakker
The Preachers
with a Golden Touch

A young couple stands together in a small studio. Television cameras, microphones, and technicians surround them. Looking directly into the eyes of millions of viewers, Jim and Tammy Bakker tell a long, sad story about their life.

They are having many financial problems. In fact, they are desperate. Without money, their television show will go off the air. They may lose their Christian ministry, as well as their house, their car, and everything else they own. Their debts are rising, and they have used up nearly all their savings. They are pleading for help—a donation of any size—from their audience.

The Bakkers produce, direct, and star in one of the most successful religious television shows in history. They are popular, fundamentalist Christian preachers, and they are millionaires. Nevertheless, Jim Bakker begins to weep.

Fundamentalists have always believed in spreading their message and converting people to their faith. Historically, fundamentalist evangelists tried to convert people through traveling ministries, or "revivals," that were held in tents and moved from town to town. The revivals featured preachers who gave stirring sermons to inspire the faithful and convert nonbelievers.

After the invention of radio and television, revivals were aired to millions of people all over the United States. Some broadcasts raised millions of dollars from their listeners and viewers. Other broadcasts failed when fundamentalist preachers fell into scandal over their private lives.

In the 1960s, as television brought the ministries of Billy Graham, Oral Roberts, and Rex Humbard directly into the home, the traveling revivals faded. The crowds in the tents were smaller, and the converts fewer. But many preachers were still driving from town to town, spreading the Christian gospel and barely earning a living. Few of them were as poor as Jim and Tammy Bakker.

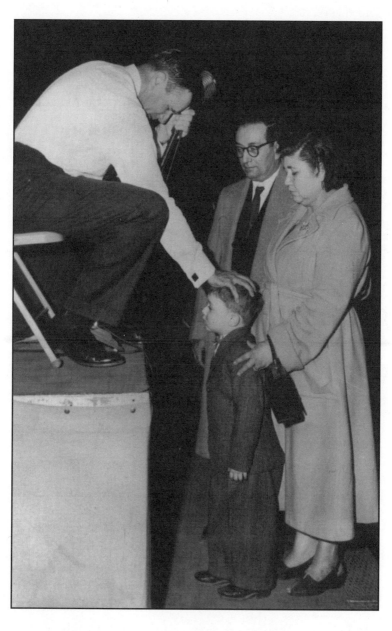

*Appearing before a 1958 audience in West
Hempstead, New York, evangelist Oral Roberts
(on stage) prays with a family.*

125

The Bakkers had met at North Central Bible College in Minneapolis, and both were Pentecostal. Pentecostals believe that the Holy Spirit works directly through them. They see life as a constant struggle between Christ and Satan. Evil forces bring on sickness and disease; the Holy Spirit heals through faith. At their services, Pentecostals believe they can communicate directly with the Holy Spirit by going into a trance and "speaking in tongues"—using a language that no one can understand.

Jim Bakker grew up in Muskegon, Michigan, the son of an auto-shop owner. While driving his car one wintry night, he accidentally ran over a small boy who was playing in the snow. The boy was rushed to the hospital. Shaken, Jim came to believe that the accident was an important sign. The boy survived, and Jim swore to recognize this miracle by devoting himself to the church.

Tammy Faye LaValley was from International Falls, a small town in northern Minnesota. Tammy and her parents belonged to a very strict Pentecostal church whose members strongly disapproved of divorce, as well as alcohol, moviegoing, jewelry, and makeup. After Tammy's parents divorced, many members of the church rejected her.

Soon after Jim and Tammy met in Minneapolis, they fell in love. They knew they wanted to spend the rest of their lives together, but North Central Bible College didn't allow marriage between students. Although Jim and Tammy were devoted to their studies, they dropped out of school and married on April Fools' Day, 1961.

Like many young married couples, the Bakkers were undecided about their future. But they were determined to stay involved with the Pentecostal church. Their lives soon changed when they met Dr. Samuel Coldstone, a traveling preacher. Dr. Coldstone was trying to raise money for a missionary project in the forests of the Amazon in South America. The Bakkers joined Dr. Coldstone's revivals and, by preaching in many revival tents, helped him to raise thousands of dollars for the project.

One day, however, the Bakkers arrived at a meeting only to discover that Dr. Coldstone had disappeared. He had taken nearly all of the money that had been raised for his missionary project.

A fellow minister whom they had trusted had tricked the Bakkers, and they were crushed. They had very little money and no friends to help them out. Nevertheless, they decided to carry on their ministry. They bought a car with their savings and hit the road.

The Bakkers lived for the next several years as wandering Pentecostal preachers. They ate and slept wherever they could. They spoke at revivals, telling stories from the Bible and helping the faithful to heal their illnesses.

After a time, they had enough money to buy a trailer that could serve as a home. Shortly after they bought it, however, the trailer broke free of their car and crashed into a telephone pole. They had no room for the night, but Jim and Tammy had to carry on their meeting. When they explained to their audience that their only home and shelter had been wrecked, they began to weep on stage. The members of the audience opened their wallets and purses and gave generously.

Their success that night was a revelation to the Bakkers, and it changed their performances. Instead of simply reading and teaching from the Bible, they began to talk openly about their private lives and struggles. The worse their situation and the more pitiful their stories, the more money the audience would drop into the collection plate. Instead of giving to a church or a mission, revival audiences were now helping an inspired young couple.

This led the Bakkers to a new fundamentalist teaching: "prosperity theology." According to the Bakkers, Christianity was not a religion of the poor and humble. Instead, money, possessions, and success were the rewards for believing in God. Outward wealth, therefore, was a sign of faith, honesty, and good works. In turn, if a Christian gave generously to his church, he or she would be rewarded by the mysterious workings of God and the Holy Spirit.

In 1965, the Bakkers joined the Christian Broadcasting Network (CBN), a television network based in Portsmouth, Virginia. Pat Robertson, another ambitious fundamentalist minister, had founded CBN as an all-religious broadcasting system. The Bakkers offered Robertson a children's show, in which they would use hand puppets to relate stories from the Bible. Jim Bakker also convinced CBN to let him do the "700 Club," a talk show that imitated Johnny Carson's "Tonight Show."

The "700 Club" became the most popular show on Robertson's network. Instead of preaching in a drafty church or in a stuffy outdoor revival tent, Jim and Tammy now sat comfortably in a TV studio, telling stories and interviewing guests. Sometimes Tammy would sing a gospel song. They asked viewers to become part of the "Club" by sending money each month to support the network and the Bakkers' ministry.

While hosting the "700 Club," Jim Bakker discovered that he had a very special talent: the ability to raise vast sums of money. His audience enjoyed the interviews, which were less formal and often more interesting than televised sermons. Viewers didn't mind sending in a few dollars every month to keep the "700 Club" on the air, and Jim Bakker quickly became one of the most popular televangelists in the country. Money from thousands of viewers poured into the "700 Club" and into Robertson's network.

Yet the Bakkers' astounding success had a dark side. The Bakkers had suffered many years of poverty, and now they were making up for the hard times by buying expensive houses, cars, and jewelry. Prosperity theology seemed to be working. But because they were spending

Pat Robertson, founder of the Christian Broadcasting Network, gave Jim Bakker his first job on television.

more than they were taking in, they always needed bigger audiences and bigger contributions.

In 1972, the Bakkers told Pat Robertson that God wanted them to quit CBN. They moved to California, where they joined another religious network and created a new show called PTL (for "Praise the Lord"). Within a year, however, they left California for Charlotte, North Carolina, where PTL continued on a local television station. By the mid-1970s, a broadcast satellite was carrying the "PTL Show" to stations nationwide, and the Bakkers were riding a new wave in broadcasting known as cable television.

Cable TV was creating thousands of new stations in hundreds of cities. With few new shows in production, however, most of these stations needed programming. Because local governments required the stations to run public-service segments, many cable systems offered inexpensive—or free—broadcast time to religious shows.

In 1978, the Bakkers launched the PTL Satellite Network, which quickly became a very big business. By renting time on a broadcast satellite, the Bakkers could beam their program directly to cable stations. In addition, they could sell their satellite time to other religious shows or to advertisers. By the mid-1980s, the PTL ministry was being shown on 1,200 cable systems, with an audience of more than 10 million cable subscribers.

At the same time, the Bakkers were receiving money from PTL members, each of whom was sending in at least $15 a month to support the ministry. Through their broadcasts, the Bakkers persuaded hundreds of thousands of people to join the PTL Club. Every month, millions of dollars poured into the offices of the PTL Satellite Network.

But their success also carried the seeds of failure. Jim was taking big risks by starting new, expensive projects without having enough money to pay for them. He often appeared on the "PTL Show" and tearfully begged for more money from the audience to keep the show running. The money usually arrived just in time. But as soon as one crisis was over, another would begin. Deep down, Jim Bakker enjoyed running dangerous financial risks; he felt they were tests of his faith.

The Bakkers' marriage was suffering as well. In the late 1970s, Tammy had made friends with a country singer named Gary Paxton. The friendship grew too close for Jim, however. To win his wife back, he tried to make her jealous by arranging to meet an attractive church secretary named Jessica Hahn in a Florida hotel. Although Tammy stayed with her husband for years afterward, Jim's meeting with Jessica Hahn would later come back to haunt him.

In the mid-1980s, Jim Bakker came up with the boldest idea of his life. Under his direction, PTL would design and build a Christian theme park called Heritage USA. Covering 2,300 acres, the park would offer amusement, accommodation, and inspiration to the vast PTL audience. There would be a water slide, miniature trains, a petting zoo, and an indoor shopping center. Visitors could also stay in the Heritage Grand Hotel. Jim dreamed that Heritage USA would rival Disney World in popularity. The PTL audience pledged millions for its construction, and the park rose quickly on a site near Charlotte.

In addition to the hotel, shopping center, and amusement park, Heritage USA boasted an elaborate broadcasting studio. Three satellite dishes beamed the PTL program to its network of cable stations. As the show went out, the money rolled in. Every day, mail vans arrived with sacks of checks, money orders, and cash at a heavily guarded counting room near the studio. During busy periods, the staff worked through the night opening

Jim Bakker, generally likeable during his public appearances, delivers flowers to a sick friend.

mail and counting donations. In the morning, armored cars arrived to transport the money to a nearby bank.

To raise even more money for the park, the Bakkers created a plan to sell "Lifetime Partnerships." For a contribution of at least $1,000, Lifetime Partners had the right to stay at the Heritage Grand Hotel for three nights every year for the rest of their lives. There was only one drawback: The hotel did not have enough rooms to accommodate all of the lifetime partners.

Nevertheless, the Lifetime Partnerships were a roaring success. By 1987, more than 100,000 people had signed up. Fame and television had put the Bakkers into the public eye, which could be uncomfortable and even frightening. Newspapers and magazines published critical stories, and the Bakkers received death threats and angry phone calls and letters. Eventually, Jim hired several bodyguards for round-the-clock protection. The heavy security cut off the Bakkers from their public as well as their staff.

By this time, the "PTL Show" was running day and night, and it seemed like contributions from PTL's 500,000 subscribers would never dry up. In the Heritage USA studios, Jim interviewed guests, Tammy sang, and both bore witness to their faith. To offer PTL viewers something more for their contributions, the Bakkers sold books, records, souvenirs, and a $675 Tammy doll.

The Bakkers owned a million-dollar home in South Carolina and several other luxurious residences. They drove a fleet of expensive cars, including a Rolls-Royce and a Mercedes. Tammy, who ignored the Pentecostal prohibition of makeup and jewelry, spent huge amounts on clothes and fashion accessories. Even their dogs lived well: Tammy had arranged for air-conditioning to be installed in their doghouse and staged an elaborate wedding ceremony for one of her pets.

The PTL network and Heritage USA quickly became the envy of other televangelists, who coveted the Bakkers' fundraising network. Jimmy Swaggert, a Pentecostal preacher from Louisiana, and Jerry Falwell, a Baptist minister with his own Christian television show, became more interested in the PTL network in early 1987, when word began leaking that the ministry was in serious financial trouble.

Rumors were flying about the huge salaries the Bakkers were paying themselves and about their expensive cars, homes, and houseboats. At the same time, several newspapers, including the *Charlotte Observer*, claimed that Jim Bakker's aides had arranged a large payment to Jessica Hahn. In return for $265,000, she was to remain silent about her 1980 meeting with him. Jim claimed the newspaper story was the work of the devil, but his meeting with Hahn—which he didn't deny—outraged many of his followers. The PTL Club began to lose thousands of its members and their monthly donations.

Sensing trouble, the Bakkers arranged to pay themselves nearly $3 million in bonuses. Soon the PTL's mounting debts pushed the organization into even worse shape, and construction of a second hotel came to a halt. Falwell asked to meet Bakker, saying he wanted to protect PTL from a takeover by Jimmy Swaggert. In March 1987, Falwell and Bakker made a deal: Bakker would step down as the leader of PTL, and Falwell would temporarily take over the ministry.

The Bakkers left Heritage USA and moved to their home in California. For several months, Falwell tried to save PTL with round-the-clock televised pleas for money.

Jealous of the Bakkers' success, Jimmy Swaggert planned to gain control of the PTL.

Jessica Hahn with her attorney, Dominic Barbara

But his efforts were in vain. The ministry was losing about $3 million a month, and in the summer of 1987 PTL declared itself bankrupt.

Although the Bakkers wanted to return to PTL, Falwell was still running the ministry. Jim Bakker had suspected all along that Falwell's real goal was to take over PTL, close it down, sell its property, and make a profit. His suspicions now seemed to be coming true. Falwell refused to let the Bakkers return to their television show or to Heritage USA. Going on ABC's "Nightline" show, Bakker called Falwell a liar and a thief. The Bakkers demanded a pension of $400,000 a year and the use of a maid and a secretary, but Falwell refused their request.

The Bakkers faced worse trouble. The FBI had been investigating the PTL organization and discovered that Jim Bakker had used money sent by PTL's Lifetime Partners not for hotel construction, as had been promised, but for PTL's operating expenses. In addition, the FBI found that PTL had paid the Bakkers and their aides enormous salaries. The Bakkers had committed fraud by raising money for one purpose and then using it to enrich themselves. Furthermore, because they had collected their donations through the mail, they had committed mail fraud.

After the large salaries and tangled finances came to light, the government's tax department decided that PTL was neither a charity nor a church. Instead, it was a

At a 1987 news conference, Jerry Falwell tells reporters that he will head the PTL after Jim Bakker's resignation.

for-profit business and subject to ordinary laws and taxes. In June 1989, the Bakkers received a tax bill for more than $1 million. After Falwell resigned as PTL's chairman, the organization collapsed.

The trial of Jim Bakker began in August 1989. Although he pled not guilty, the government easily proved its case against him by using many of Bakker's former co-workers, aides, and friends as witnesses. At one point, Bakker suffered a nervous breakdown, falling to the floor in a nearby office and cowering in terror from the police. The jury felt little sympathy for Bakker and found him guilty. The judge sentenced Bakker to 45 years in prison and gave him a $500,000 fine. (In 1992, a federal judge reduced Bakker's sentence to 8 years.)

The Bakkers and PTL were finished, but it wasn't to be the final scandal for televangelists. Jimmy Swaggert and Oral Roberts have had their own financial and personal problems, too. Many religious leaders still criticize Jerry Falwell for his role in the PTL affair. Yet Falwell, as well as Pat Robertson and the Christian Broadcasting Network, remain powerful Christian institutions. The PTL scandal destroyed the faith of some people. For others, religion is still big business.

In 1992, three years after her husband was sentenced to prison, Tammy Faye Bakker filed for divorce.

A Chronology of Con

1596 British pirate Sir Francis Drake dies

1861 The U.S. Civil War begins (ends in 1865)

1866 British writer H.G. Wells is born

1868 A man identifying himself as Lord Glencairn swindles Marshall and Son jewelry shop in Edinburgh, Scotland

1871 Scottish hustler Lord Gordon-Gordon— formerly known as Lord Glencairn—arrives in the United States and continues his life of crime

1872 Lord Gordon-Gordon secretly heads for Canada after his trial begins in the United States

1873 Instead of surrendering to the police, Lord Gordon-Gordon kills himself

1877 Scientists discover grooves on the surface of
Mars, which some believe to be the work of
intelligent life forms

**Carlo Ponzi (later called *Charles*) is born in
Italy**

**Chicago con man Joseph Weil is born—but
years later claims to have been born in 1875**

1896 Joseph Weil's favorite comic strip, *Hogan's Alley*—
featuring a character called "Yellow Kid"—first
appears in the *New York World*

1898 *The War of the Worlds*, H.G. Wells's book about
Martian invaders, is published

1903 **Italian immigrant Charles Ponzi arrives in the
United States, where he works in the wholesale
food business**

1905 Business tycoon Howard Hughes is born in
Houston, Texas

1908 **Carlo Ponzi—using the alias "Bianchi "— is
arrested for forgery in Canada**

**Plainclothes policeman Fred "Deacon"
Buckminster meets Joseph Weil, which
begins their 20-year partnership in crime**

1914 World War I begins (ends in 1918)

1915 Actor Orson Welles is born in Kenosha, Wisconsin

1919 Sudie B. Whiteaker and Milo Lewis con Oscar Hartzell of Madison County, Iowa, into believing he is an heir of Sir Francis Drake

1920 Charles Ponzi's crooked Securities Exchange Company is a success—but still $4 million in debt

1921 Oscar Hartzell tells friends that he knows the heir of Sir Francis Drake

1924 Oscar Hartzell, now head of the Sir Francis Drake Association, leaves the United States for England, claiming that he will look into the Drake inheritance

Charles Ponzi is released from one prison and sentenced to another

1929 The U.S. stock market crashes, sending the nation into the Great Depression

1933 Oscar Hartzell is deported from England and sentenced to prison in the United States

1934 Charles Ponzi is deported from the United States and gets a job in the Italian financial department of Benito Mussolini—where he secretly steals from the treasury

Orson Welles makes his stage and radio debut

1937 The nation panics when the *Hindenburg* aircraft catches fire, crashes, and kills more than 30 people while trying to land in Lakehurst, New Jersey

1938 The nation panics when Orson Welles performs "The War of the Worlds" radio broadcast about Martians invading Grovers Mill, New Jersey

1939 World War II begins (ends in 1945)

1940 Jim Bakker is born in Muskegon, Michigan

1941 Orson Welles writes, directs and stars in his first film, the highly successful *Citizen Kane*

1942 After getting out of prison, hustler Joseph Weil decides to go straight

Tammy Faye LaValley is born in International Falls, Minnesota

1946 H.G. Wells, author of *The War of the Worlds*, dies—eight years after Orson Welles's chilling radio adaption of the novel

1948 Joseph Weil writes his autobiography, *Yellow Kid Weil*

1949 Charles Ponzi dies in the charity ward of a Rio de Janeiro hospital

1961 Jim Bakker marries Tammy Faye LaValley

1965 Jim and Tammy Bakker join the Christian Broadcasting Network

1969 Clifford Irving has two books published: *Spy: The Story of Modern Espionage,* and *Fake: The Story of Elmyrde Hory, the Greatest Forger of Our Time*

1970 After reading about reclusive tycoon Howard Hughes in *Newsweek* magazine, Clifford Irving comes up with his own get-rich idea

1971 Clifford Irving tells the McGraw-Hill publishing company that he will help Howard Hughes write his autobiography

1972 Clifford Irving and his accomplices are
sentenced to prison

Jim and Tammy Bakker leave the Christian
Broadcasting Network

1973 *The Sting*, the most famous movie about
con artists in history, wins academy awards
for best picture, director, screenplay, and
song

1976 Joseph "Yellow Kid" Weil dies

Billionaire Howard Hughes dies, never having
written his autobiography

The United States launches *Viking*, the first
Earth probe to reach Mars

1978 Jim and Tammy Bakker launch the PTL
Satellite Network

1980 Jim Bakker meets 19-year-old Jessica
Hahn in a Florida hotel room

1981 *The Hoax*—Clifford Irving's tell-all book
about his attempt to outsmart McGraw-Hill—
is published

1985   After appearing in more than 60 films,
        actor Orson Welles dies

        Jim Bakker pays Jessica Hahn $265,000 to
        keep quiet about their 1980 tryst—but the
        secret eventually gets out

1987   Jim Bakker steps down as leader of the PTL, and
        minister Jerry Falwell takes his place

1989   The PTL goes bankrupt, and Jim Bakker is tried
        and sent to prison

1992   Tammy Faye Bakker divorces Jim Bakker, who
        remains behind bars

Bibliography

Brady, Frank. *Citizen Welles: A Biography of Orson Welles.* New York: Charles Scribner's Sons, 1989.

Cantril, Hadley. *The Invasion from Mars.* New York: Harper and Row, 1940.

Dunn, Donald H. *Ponzi! The Boston Swindler.* New York: McGraw-Hill, 1975.

Fay, Stephen, Lewis Chester and Magnus Linklater. *Hoax: The Inside Story of the Howard Hughes-Clifford Irving Affair.* New York: Viking Press, 1972.

Higham, Charles. *Orson Welles: The Rise and Fall of An American Genius.* New York: St. Martin's Press, 1985.

Irving, Clifford. *The Hoax.* Sagaponack, New York: The Permanent Press, 1981.

Klein, Alexander. *Grand Deception.* New York: J.B. Lippincott, 1955.

Koch, Howard. *The Panic Broadcast.* Boston: Little, Brown and Company, 1970.

Larsen, Egon. *The Deceivers.* London: John Baker, 1966.

Martz, Larry. *Ministry of Greed.* New York: Weidenfeld and Nicholson, 1988.

Nash, Jay Robert. *Hustlers and Con Men*. New York: M. Evans and Company, 1976.

Richardson, Michael. *The Edge of Disaster*. New York: St. Martin's Press, 1987.

Shepard, Charles E. *Forgiven: The Rise and Fall of Jim Bakker and the PTL Ministry*. New York: Atlantic Monthly Press, 1989.

Taylor, John Russell. *Orson Welles: A Celebration*. Boston: Little, Brown and Company, 1986.

Weil, Joseph. *Yellow Kid Weil*. Chicago: Ziff-Davis, 1948.

Index

Austin, Horace, 26, 27, 28

Bakker, Jim, 9, 122-124; background of, 126-127; and CBN, 128-129, 131; and doctrine of prosperity theology, 128, 129; early revivals of, 127-128; and Heritage USA, 132-134, 135, 136; marital problems of, 132, 141; and PTL, 131-134, 135-136, 138, 140; wealth of, 129, 131-132, 133, 134-135; resignation of, 136, 138, 139; trial of, 140

Bakker, Tammy, 9, 122-124; background of, 126-127; and CBN, 128-129, 131; and doctrine of prosperity theology, 128, 129; early revivals of, 127-128; and Heritage USA, 132-134, 135, 136; marital problems of, 132, 141; and PTL, 131-134, 135-136, 138, 140; wealth of, 129, 131-132, 133, 134-135

Banco Zarossi, 32-34

Barbara, Dominic, 137

Barron, Clarence, 43-44

Biczek, Ewald, 66

"big store," 57-58

Blake, Earl, 47

"boiler rooms," 61, 63

"bookmaking," 53, 57-58

Boston, 34, 37, 39, 40, 42, 43

Boston Globe, 46

Brackett, George, 23, 24, 25, 26, 28

Buckland, Duke of, 78, 82, 85

Buckminster, Fred "Deacon," 65, 66

Carson, Johnny, 129

Casablanca, 101

Charlotte Observer, 135

Chicago, 53, 54, 55, 58, 59, 63, 64, 67, 68, 69

Christian Broadcasting Network (CBN), 128-129, 130, 131, 140

Citizen Kane, 100

Clark, Horace, 21

Cleo, Madame, 59
Coldstone, Samuel, 127

Dietrich, Noah, 112, 113,
114, 118
Dorian, Richard, 63-64.
See also Weil, Joseph
Drake, Francis, estate of,
74-77, 79-84

Elysium Development
Company, 59-61
Erie Railroad, 15, 17, 18,
20

Falwell, Jerry, 135, 136,
138, 139, 140
FBI (Federal Bureau of
Investigation), 138
Field, David Dudley, 21-
22
Fletcher, Loren, 25
Fort Garry, 22, 23, 25, 26,
28
fundamentalists, 124, 128

gambling on horse races,
53, 55, 57-58
Glencairn, Lord, 11-12,
22. *See also* Gordon-
Gordon, Lord
Gordon-Gordon, Lord,

10, 24; background of,
17, 21-22; in Canada,
22-23, 25-26, 28-29;
and Erie Railroad
stock, 18, 20-21; in
Minneapolis, 12-14; in
New York, 15, 16-18;
suicide of, 29; trial of,
21-22
Gould, Jay, 15, 17, 18, 19,
20, 22; tricked by Lord
Gordon-Gordon, 18-
21, 29
Graham, Billy, 124
Grant, Ulysses, 16, 26
Great Depression, 81, 85
greed, 7, 8, 9, 71
Greeley, Horace, 15, 16,
17, 21
Grovers Mill, 90, 92, 93,
98, 101

Hahn, Jessica, 132, 135,
137
Hanover Trust Company,
40, 42, 44, 46
Hartzell, Canfield, 78
Hartzell, Oscar: arrest of,
82, 83; death of, 84; as
deputy sheriff, 72, 76;
and Drake estate scam,
74, 76-77, 79-83; as
Duke of Buckland, 78,

82, 85; in England, 77-80, 82; jail sentences of, 84-85

Hearth and Home, 52, 55

Hemingway, Ernest, 114

Heritage USA, 132-134, 135, 136, 138

Herring, Clyde, 99

Hitler, Adolf, 69, 70

Hogan's Alley, 56

horse racing, 53, 55, 58-59

Houseman, John, 88, 90, 101

Hoy, Mike, 23, 25, 28

Hughes, Helga, 109, 110. *See also* Irving, Edith

Hughes, Howard, 102, 104-106, 111, 116, 117, 119; "autobiography" of, 102, 107-109, 111-112, 114-116, 117, 118, 119

Hughes Aircraft Corporation, 104, 106

Hughes Tool Company, 116

Humbard, Rex, 124

Ibiza, 103, 108, 109, 114, 118, 121

Indianapolis, 65, 66

Internal Revenue Service, 43

Iowa, 74, 76, 80, 82

Irving, Clifford: and Howard Hughes "autobiography," 102, 107-109, 111-112, 114-116, 117, 119; "interviews" of, with Howard Hughes, 104, 107, 109, 111, 114, 116; and Noah Dietrich, 112, 114, 118; as novelist, 8, 103-104; prison sentence of, 119-121

Irving, Edith, 109, 110, 115, 118, 119-121

Italian immigrants in U.S., 31-32, 34

Koch, Howard, 88, 90, 95, 99, 100-101

Leavenworth Penitentiary, 67, 68, 84

Lewis, Milo, 74, 76

Life magazine, 111-112, 114, 115, 119

Loomis, John, 13-14, 15

Macdonald, John, 28

McCulloch, Frank, 116, 118

McGraw-Hill, 103, 104, 107-109, 114-116, 117, 118, 119

mail fraud, 78-79, 82, 84, 138

"mark," 8, 57, 58, 59, 65, 71

Mars, invasion from, 8, 88, 90, 92-93, 94, 95-98

Marshall and Son, 11, 12, 28, 29

Martinique, Hotel, 67

medicine show, 54-55

Mercury Theatre, 87, 92-93, 99

Meriwether, Doc, 54-55

Metropolitan Hotel, 15, 17, 22

Meyer, Stanley, 112

Minneapolis, 12-14, 16, 23, 24, 26, 126

Montreal, 32, 33, 46

Mussolini, Benito, 6, 48

New York City, 14, 15, 18, 21, 26

"Nightline," 138

New York Tribune, 15, 16

North Central Bible College, 126-127

Northern Pacific Railroad, 13-14

Osborn, Osborn and Osborn, 118

Paxton, Gary, 132

Pentecostals, 126, 127, 135

Phillips, Carl, 92

Pierson, Richard, 92, 97, 98-99

Ponzi, Charles, 6, 30; arrest of, 46; bank scheme of, 33-34; in Boston, 34-46; death of, 48; immigration of, to U.S., 32; deportation to Italy, 48; investment fraud of, 36-37, 38, 39-40, 41-43, 46, 48; jail terms of, 34, 35, 46; in Montreal, 32-34, 46; in Rio de Janeiro, 48, 49

Porter, Jim, 59-61

"premium coupons," 63-64

"Project Octavio," 108, 109, 111, 114, 115, 116, 118

prosperity theology, 128, 129

PTL ("Praise the Lord"), 131, 132, 133, 134,

135-136, 138, 140
PTL Satellite Network,
131, 132, 133, 134, 135
"pyramid game," 48

railroad industry, 13
Reuel, Henri, 68-69. *See
also* Weil, Joseph
revivals, 124, 127
Rio de Janeiro, 48, 49
Roberts, Oral, 124, 125,
140
Robertson, Pat, 128-129,
130, 131, 140
Royal Canadian Mounted
Police, 23

Salvati, Angelo, 33, 34
Scotland Yard, 12
Scott, Thomas, 17
Securities Exchange
Company (SEC), 37,
39-40, 41, 42-43, 44, 46
"700 Club," 129
shell game, 7, 8
Sir Francis Drake
Association, 76, 77, 79,
80, 85
"60 Minutes," 119
Smith, Thomas, 28
Spruce Goose, 106

"stall," 65
Suskind, Richard, 107,
109, 111, 114, 116, 119
Swaggert, Jimmy, 135,
136, 140
"switch," 65

telemarketing, 63, 69, 71
television, revivals on,
124, 128-129, 131, 134,
135, 140
three-card monte, 8
Time magazine, 121
"Tonight Show," 129

Victoria (queen of
England), 17

Wallace, Mike, 119
"War of the Worlds"
broadcast, 88, 90, 92-
93, 94, 95, 97-99, 100;
planning of, 88, 90, 95;
public reaction to, 93,
95, 99, 100, 101
War of the Worlds, The
(novel), 88, 89, 96
Weil, Joseph: background
of, 53; as bookmaker,
57-58; death of, 71;
as Richard Dorian, 63-
64; Henri Reuel, 68-69;

eyeglass swindle of, 52-53, 55; and medicine show, 54-55; nickname of, 56, 62; prison sentence of, 66-67, 69; race track swindle of, 55, 57; real estate swindle of, 59-61; as stable owner, 58-59; stock market swindles of, 61, 63, 65-66

Welles, Orson, 8, 86, 89, 91; and *Citizen Kane*, 100; and "War of the Worlds" broadcast, 87-88, 90, 95, 99, 100, 101

Wells, H.G., 88, 89, 92

Whiteaker, Sudie, 74, 76

World War I, 65

World War II, 48, 69, 101

Zarossi, Louis, 32-33

Photo Credits

Photographs courtesy of The Bettmann Archive: pp. 6, 35, 47, 49, 50, 56, 60, 62, 66, 71, 89, 96, 102, 110, 113, 117, 120, 122, 125, 130, 133, 136, 137, 139, 141; Western Canada Pictorial Index, p. 10; Library of Congress, pp. 16, 19, 70, 75, 105; Minneapolis Public Library, Special Collections, pp. 25, 27; Minnesota Historical Society, pp. 24, 26; Boston Public Library, pp. 30, 38, 41, 45; *The Leavenworth Times*, p. 68; *The Des Moines Register*, p. 72; National Archives, pp. 78, 80; The *Iowan* magazine, p. 83; Lilly Library, Indiana University, pp. 86, 91, 100; NASA, p. 94; Smithsonian Institution, p. 106.

ABOUT THE AUTHOR

TOM STREISSGUTH, born in Washington, D.C., in 1958, attended Yale University as a student of history, literature, languages, and music. He has travelled widely in Europe and the Middle East, and has worked as a teacher, editor, and journalist. Streissguth is the author of *Soviet Leaders from Lenin to Gorbachev*, *International Terrorists*, and the forthcoming book, *Charismatic Cult Leaders*. He lives in Minneapolis with his wife and daughter.